ADVENTUROUS PUB WALKS
IN
HAMPSHIRE & THE NEW FOREST

Nick Channer

COUNTRYSIDE BOOKS

NEWBURY, BERKSHIRE

First published 2004
© Nick Channer 2004

COUNTRYSIDE BOOKS
3 Catherine Road
Newbury, Berkshire

To view our complete range of books,
please visit us at
www.countrysidebooks.co.uk

ISBN 1 85306 834 9

Designed by Peter Davies, Nautilus Design
Photographs by the author

Produced through MRM Associates Ltd., Reading
Typeset by Mac Style Ltd, Scarborough, N. Yorkshire
Printed by Woolnough Bookbinding Ltd., Irthlingborough

CONTENTS

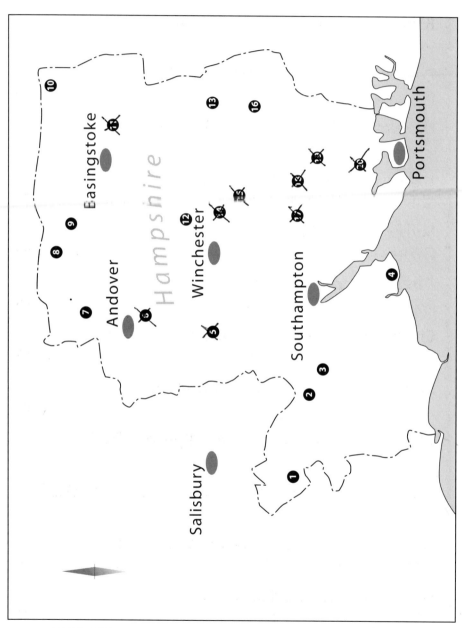

AREA MAP SHOWING THE LOCATION OF THE WALKS

INTRODUCTION

Hampshire is just the place for adventurous walks – as I have been lucky enough to find out. Having completed the final walk for this book, I drove home along the county's rural back roads that are still largely traffic-free. The journey required careful negotiation as well as expert navigation from my passenger but, above all, it underlined Hampshire's vastness and its huge potential for adventurous walking. Studying our route home on the Ordnance Survey map, my attention was drawn to a complex network of paths and tracks criss-crossing the landscape, shooting off in all directions as far as the eye can see. No one could deny it is a county made for walking.

If you are not familiar with Hampshire, it is the sheer size and scale of it that catches you by surprise. Compared with neighbouring Berkshire to the north, it is huge and within its boundaries lies a bewildering variety of scenery. Everything the walker and country lover could possibly want is here. With its scenic coastline, charming villages, rolling farmland and spectacular forests and woodland, much of it conveys a sense of space, distance and quiet beauty. In many parts of Hampshire you can escape the pressures of modern life and enter a world of green fields, hidden valleys and wide, windswept landscapes where you might not meet another living soul.

The walks in this guide are aimed at those wanting more than a casual stroll or a gentle jaunt to the pub. Ranging in distance from 7 to 12 miles, they are intended to be a little more challenging, providing hours of pleasure and stimulating a real sense of achievement. With a range of visitor attractions and numerous other diversions and distractions, you should allow the whole day to complete many of the routes. It is advisable to take a copy of the relevant Ordnance Survey map with you, too, as well as some form of comfortable waterproof clothing and a good pair of boots. Remember, the weather can change suddenly and you are likely to be in the great outdoors for much of the day. The New Forest is a good example of how woodland paths and rides can become sodden with rain.

One thing that goes hand in hand with walking is the classic British pub. No country walk is complete without the chance to savour and enjoy a decent pint of beer and something to eat. I have tried to devise as many walks as I can, with a pub actually on the route rather than at the finish. Part of the enjoyment of the hike is looking forward to rest and refreshment midway round the walk. Routes 2 and 5 have hostelries at the finish of the route and Walk 12 begins at a pub where permission has been given to use the car park. A number of establishments in the guide are open all day so you won't need to worry about rushing to beat closing time. Telephone numbers and details of food and drink are also included.

It is 25 years since I wrote my first walking guide and in that time I have trekked across much of Britain earning a living from my travels but regarding it more as a way of life than a job. I count myself extremely lucky. Over the years, many parts of the country have become firm favourites and I am often asked if there is a particular county I am drawn to more than any other. I think I would have to say that Hampshire is probably top of my list. After all, I have written about it extensively and I've had a long time to get to know it.

Happy walking!

Nick Channer

MARTIN AND BOKERLEY DITCH

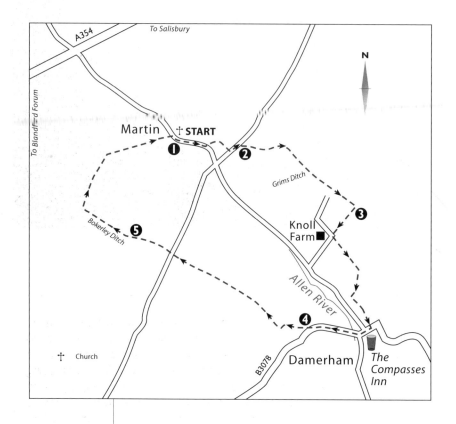

Distance:
10¹/₄ miles

Starting point:
The car park by
Martin church. GR
068195

Map: OS Landranger 184 or OS Outdoor Leisure 22

How to get there: *Martin is signposted off the A354
Salisbury to Blandford road. The church is in the village
centre.*

THE COMPASSES AT DAMERHAM

*I*t should come as no surprise that the remote downland country explored by this spectacular walk is sometimes referred to as Hampshire's wild west or the Western Front. This is a corner of the county where you can savour a real sense of ancient history. Starting in the sleepy village of Martin, the route soon makes for high ground where there are breathtaking views in all directions. Enjoy a welcome break at the Compasses pub in Damerham before following the walk across country to Bokerley Ditch, a lengthy earthwork frontier.

Situated next to the cricket pitch in Damerham, the **Compasses Inn** is a 400-year-old coaching house with plenty of character and charm in the pine furnished bars. Look out for an impressive collection of malt whiskies. The menu is interesting and varied with locally produced fresh food, light snacks and fish. The pub is also known throughout the area for its cheeses served with home-made pickles. Compasses Ale, Ringwood Best and Hop Back Summer Lightning are among the beers. Overnight accommodation is available too. Telephone: 01725 518231.

 The Walk

Until 1895 the parish of Martin was in Wiltshire. The village has changed little since those days and it remains one of the region's most isolated communities. The antiquary and folklorist John Aubrey wrote: 'I take Martin to be the best seated for healthy airs etc and sports of any place in the county'. The River Allen used to run down the village street in winter; these days it disappears underground through a culvert.

① From the car park walk down to the main street in **Martin** and turn left. Avoid a turning for **East Martin** and continue towards **Fordingbridge**. Look for a footpath on the left, by a 30 mile per hour speed restriction sign, and follow it to a field. Go up the slope, heading towards the wooded horizon, keeping to the left of the hedge in front of you. Turn left on reaching a lane and follow it towards some barns. (1 mile)

② Veer half-right at the fingerpost and follow the path between fences to a field. Continue ahead, keeping to the left boundary, and on reaching the first corner, by trees and bushes, go straight on along a narrow path running alongside the fence. Briefly cross a field and look for a gap in the undergrowth. Just beyond it is a footpath sign. Turn left here and follow the field edge towards some pylons. Go round the corner to a junction of tracks and continue ahead, keeping the boundary on your left. Head for a plantation ahead and follow the path along the woodland edge, climbing gradually. Aim for a stile and gate, cross into the field and turn right. Make for the next stile and follow the woodland boundary to a right-hand stile. (1³/₄ miles)

③ Cross over and take the track down through some trees to **Knoll Farm**. Turn left in front of a cottage and follow the track to a barrier. Continue through the trees, keeping to the track as it curves to the right and down to a junction. Keep left here and walk to the road. Cross over into **West Park Lane** and walk along to the next junction. You are now in the centre of the village of **Damerham**, with the **Compasses Inn** on the left. The walk turns right to the **River Allen**. Pass the village **High Street** and follow the road towards **Cranborne**. Ignore a turning for **Rockbourne** and **Martin**, pass a track on the right and continue for a few yards to the next turning on the right – **Boulsbury Lane**. (2$^1/_2$ miles)

④ Turn right here, then continue round a right-hand bend and go straight on along a bridleway when the lane sweeps to the left. Pass

between sprawling farm outbuildings and keep ahead to the next road. Continue on the bridleway, head up the slope to a gate on the right and veer half-left for **Bokerley Ditch**, avoiding the path running ahead to **Martin**. (2$^1/_2$ miles)

Constructed by the Romano-British in the 4th century AD, Bokerley Ditch is an impressive earthwork frontier between Hampshire and Dorset – the longest in the county. Running for 4 miles as a bank and ditch along the county boundary, in places Bokerley Ditch is 100 ft wide and 15 ft high. Even today it

OPEN DOWNLAND ON THE HAMPSHIRE BORDER

is an impressive feature in this desolate landscape.

⑤ Keep to the left of the trees on the skyline and look for a stile in the corner of the field. Pass a nature reserve sign for **Martin Down** and follow the path as it runs alongside **Bokerley Ditch**. On reaching a track turn right, heading away from the earthwork. Pass to the right of the car park, merge with another track and follow it into **Martin**. Turn right at the road, then left for the car park where the walk began. (2¹/₂ miles)

THE CHURCH IN MARTIN

 Date walk completed:

FRITHAM IN THE NEW FOREST

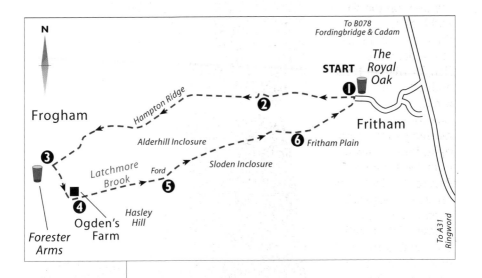

Distance:
9¹/₂ miles

Starting point:
The car park near the Royal Oak at Fritham.
GR 231139

Map: OS Landranger 195 or OS Outdoor Leisure 22

How to get there: *Take the B3078 between Fordingbridge and junction 1 of the M27 at Cadnam and follow the signs for Fritham. Alternatively, turn off the A31 between Cadnam and Ringwood and follow the village signs.*

FRITHAM

*T*his corner of the New Forest was once home to a gunpowder plant. The Schultze factory, which depended on local sulphur, charcoal and saltpetre, was founded in the mid 1860s and produced gunpowder during the First World War. However, you wouldn't know it today as you stroll through the region's woodland glades and sunny clearings. All signs of industry have long gone. This walk takes you through the famous inclosures to the heart of the New Forest and once you are away from the roads and car parks, you can often walk for miles without seeing anyone.

Little changed in 100 years or so, Fritham's **Royal Oak** is a tiny pub deep in the forest. From the outside it looks more like a house than an inn and its position down a quiet lane on the edge of a scattered community makes it quite difficult to find. This is definitely not a pub where you'll find fruit machines or juke boxes. Expect, instead, civilised conversation and parties of walkers and ramblers savouring the prospect of a long hike in the forest. During the winter, cosy fires add to the inviting atmosphere and in this attractive setting you can enjoy the likes of ploughman's lunches and home-baked quiche. The popular garden has pretty views. Ringwood Best, Hop Back Summer Lightning and Cheriton Village Elder are among the real ales. Telephone: 02380 812606.

 *The Walk*

The New Forest is the jewel in Hampshire's crown. It is the largest remaining unspoilt medieval forest in western Europe and has a unique atmosphere and a distinctive character. Once a royal preserve, it is a place of ancient dark legends and historic literary associations. The word 'forest' conjures up images of wild, uncultivated tracts of land and extensive dense woodland. In medieval times that is precisely how the New Forest was made up. Today, apart from the obvious intrusion of 21st century commercialism, the forest has changed little since William the Conqueror established it as his deer park. Comprising more than 90,000 acres, extending roughly from the south coast to the Wiltshire border, the variety of landscape is immense and among the many tree species are beech, oak and chestnut.

① On leaving the car park, take the drive to the road. On the left is a famous post box, erected by the Schultze works prior to 1900 and restored by the Forestry Commission in 1976. Retrace your steps for a few yards, then veer right to follow the cycle route to **Frogham**. Keep right at the next fork and stay on the obvious track as it meanders through the forest. (1 mile)

② Cross over a stream to reach a fork, keep left at this point and continue following the waymarked cycle route. Further on the track ascends to higher ground, finally emerging from the trees to cross heath and open plain – a typical New Forest landscape. This is **Hampton Ridge**. Keep left at the next fork and follow the track between gorse bushes and bracken. A familiar triangulation pillar can be seen over on the right along this open, exposed stretch of the walk. (2 miles)

③ Keep an eye out for the houses of **Frogham** up ahead in the trees and continue on the track to reach the road on a U-bend. Keep left and pass **Abbots Well**, identified by two drinking holes – one for humans, the other for animals. If you wish to break the journey at this point follow the road to the **Foresters Arms** and then, suitably fed and watered, return to the bend. Otherwise, turn left at the sign 'no public access – private residences only' and follow the track alongside **Ogdens Farm**. (2 miles)

④ Make for a ford and cross it via a footbridge. Keep left at the fork beyond it and follow the track. As you approach a T-junction, with a bungalow visible just beyond it, turn left and follow a path by clusters of gorse bushes and brambles. Head for a gap in the line of bushes ahead and then swing a little to the left, keeping well to the left of **Hasley Hill**. Follow the path parallel to **Latchmore Brook**, remain on the broad, grassy ride and ultimately it narrows to a thin strip bordered by bracken. (2 miles)

THE ROYAL OAK

A DELIGHTFUL PATH NEAR FRITHAM

⑤ Eventually you reach a fence corner; keep left just beyond it at the fork, following the woodland ride between the trees of **Alderhill Inclosure**. Approach some fencing and a cross-track and avoid a path and footbridge on the left. Keep to the clear path through **Sloden Inclosure** and a parallel track is seen on the right through the trees. Cross a footbridge and continue over a junction of paths. (1¹/₂ miles)

⑥ Follow the path out of the woods and through a spacious clearing, climbing gradually between oak, holly and bracken. Cross a path and continue climbing to merge with a wider path. Avoid the left turning into the trees at the fork and keep right, striding out now over **Fritham Plain**. The woodland is a short distance away on the left. On reaching a clear track, keep left and head towards **Fritham**. Return to the car park on the outskirts of the village. (1 mile)

With a handful of houses and a tiny pub, Fritham is little more than a hamlet at the heart of the New Forest. But it was a very different scene in the middle of the 19th century when the German Eduard Schultze founded his famous gunpowder factory here. During the early years, the factory produced gunpowder for the Prussian army in the 1870 Franco-Prussian War. The site covered quite an extensive area and, by the turn of the century, something in the order of 70 men were employed during daylight hours, with a similar number working the night-shift. They earned £1 a week and some of them slogged six miles or more to work, which began every day at about 7 am. The factory was well-known in its day and the name and product have remained in the public consciousness. There is even an entry for Schultze in the Oxford English Dictionary. The definition reads: 'gunpowder, an explosive having nitrolignin as its chief constituent, first made in England in 1863'. The factory eventually closed in 1921. About the time the gunpowder factory was starting up, Fritham's first school opened, built on forest land outside the village. Before this, pupils had to walk to neighbouring Bramshaw and back every day – an unknown experience for many of today's children.

 Date walk completed:

LYNDHURST HILL AND CONAN DOYLE'S GRAVE AT MINSTEAD

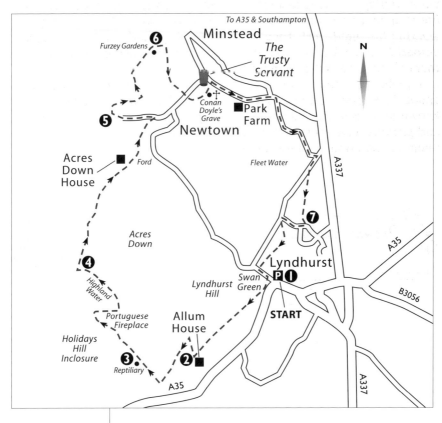

Distance:
11 miles

Starting point:
The car park at Swan Green, Lyndhurst. GR 288083

Map: OS Landranger 195 & 196 and OS Outdoor Leisure 22

How to get there: From Lyndhurst take the A35 towards Christchurch and turn right at Swan Green. The car park is on the left.

THE PORTUGUESE FIREPLACE

*O*ne of the loveliest walks anywhere in William the Conqueror's Nova Foresta, this lengthy hike begins on the outskirts of Lyndhurst and before long stumbles on a fascinating relic of the First World War. Further on, it passes Furzey Gardens, one of the region's most popular attractions, before reaching the graves of Sir Arthur Conan Doyle and his wife in a quiet corner of a quintessentially English churchyard.

The first thing to catch your eye as you arrive at the **Trusty Servant** in Minstead is the interesting and unusual verse by the main door, explaining the inn's name. Above it is a copy of an original 16th century picture belonging to Winchester College whose school magazine is known as *The Trusty Servant*. Among the main dishes in the bar are pan-roasted breast of duck, medallions of beef, tenderloin of pork, fillet steak, omelettes, filled jacket potatoes, ploughman's lunches, Gloucester sausages, liver and bacon, home-cooked ham, lasagne and double eggs and chips. Vegetarian dishes are also available. The Trusty Servant is open all day with food available throughout that time. Real ales include Gale's HSB and Flowers. Telephone: 02380 812137.

The Walk

① From the car park, go diagonally across the green, heading towards the bottom corner near the main A35. About 60 yards before reaching it, cross a ditch and head for a wide path running up **Lyndhurst Hill** between trees and margins of undergrowth. The main road runs parallel on the left. Pass between holly, oak and beech trees and continue for some time, eventually reaching a walled garden on the left. (1¼ miles)

Allum House beyond the garden was once the home of the Fenwick family, who donated the hospital of the same name at Lyndhurst. The hospital crops up towards the end of the walk.

② On reaching **Corner Cottage**, swing right and head for a seat. Keep right and follow the path to a junction. Turn left here and avoid a path on the right. Descend the hill, merge with another path, and keep ahead. Cross a stream and turn right at the junction. Follow the firm track and soon reach a cottage on the right. Just beyond it lies the entrance to the **Reptiliary** at **Holidays Hill Inclosure**. (1 mile)

Established in 1972, the aim of the site is to help small creatures to survive by providing a breeding reserve. The sand lizard is one such creature.

③ From the **Reptiliary**, head for the car park and turn right at a sign 'We hope you enjoyed your visit'. Follow the track away from the site and keep right at a junction. On reaching the road, turn right, and walk along to the **Portuguese Fireplace** on the right.

To the casual observer or the speeding motorist, this might seem like no more than a block of flint situated beside the road. On closer inspection, you can see it is something a little more unusual. The Portuguese Fireplace, neglected and at the mercy of the elements, stands on the site of a hutted camp, occupied by a Portuguese army unit during the First World War. This region of Hampshire played a key role in the war effort and the local workforce was greatly helped by the unit. Its members were involved in producing timber in local lumber camps. The fireplace comes from the old cookhouse and serves as a memorial to the men who lived and worked here almost a century ago.

Follow the road and turn left at the sign for **Millyford Bridge**. Pass through the barrier and keep to the left of the parking area. From here, begin following the track through extensive woodland, passing over the **Highland Water**. Cross a second footbridge to reach an intersection after about 150 yards. (1½ miles)

④ Turn right here and stay on the track as it narrows to a path, passing through a wooden gate. Cross another footbridge, pass through a clearing and, before long, you come

MINSTEAD CHURCH

to a track on a bend. Go straight ahead, passing the car park for **Acres Down**. Join a lane at **Acres Down Farm** and follow it to a ford. Pass between fields, following the road alongside **Robins Bush Farm**, and at the next crossroads go straight over to follow a lane. On reaching the next junction by a post box and telephone box, turn left, and then left again after several paces. Follow the secluded bridleway through the trees and at length you reach the road. (1³/₄ miles)

⑤ Keep right, then take the track on the right, after a few yards. Keep left at the fork and pass a house called **Skymers**. When the track bends right by the next house, go straight on into the trees. Turn sharp right at the junction and follow the track down to a bend in the road. Take the waymarked path on the left and cut between fencing and hedges. Descend to the corner of a field, where there is a footbridge. Cross a tree-lined field to a stile, turn right, and make your way down through the trees to a footbridge. Keep right at the waymarked junction, cross another footbridge, and head for a gate. Keep slightly left here and climb the hill to **Furzey Gardens**. This 8-acre site includes a 16th century cottage and a gallery, selling the work of local craftsmen. The gardens are open every day throughout the year. (1¹/₂ miles)

⑥ Turn right and walk along the lane, taking the first turning on the right. Follow the road to the ford at **Newtown** and, at the junction, turn left, then right at the sign 'access only to Petershold Farm'. Take the waymarked path through the kissing gate and up through the trees. Further on, you reach **Minstead church**.

The church includes private pews with their own fireplace, built for the residents of Castle Malwood, a large house nearby. It is even said that dinner was brought in through a private doorway. The church is also renowned in the area for its striking three-decker pulpit.

The churchyard here is the final resting place of Sir Arthur Conan Doyle and his wife, Jean. They lived at nearby Bignell Wood, north of the A31, and he included Minstead in one of his stories 'The White Company'. Best known for creating the most famous fictional sleuth in history, Sherlock Holmes, Conan Doyle set himself up as a GP in the Hampshire town of Southsea before an annual allowance from his first wife, Louisa, gave him the freedom to write. Holmes made his debut in 'A Study in Scarlet', which features the old Netley hospital, now gone, on the banks of Southampton Water. Towards the end of his life, Conan Doyle became increasingly

23

THE INN SIGN FOR THE TRUSTY SERVANT

obsessed with spiritualism, following the death of his son, Kingsley, from influenza in 1918.

Turn right at the junction and pass **Park Farm**. Continue along **Lyndhurst Road**, passing a turning on the left, and swing right at the sign 'access to Williams Hill'. On reaching the farm, go straight on, cross the **Fleet Water** and then swing left to reach the road. Turn right and follow the road until you approach a house on the left. Look for the remains of a fallen tree here and take the path into woodland, keeping roughly parallel to the road. Now look for a stream away to the left and take the path running down to it. Cross over and swing right, up the bank. Veer right at the fork at the top, emerging from the trees to skirt a clearing for a few yards. Continue through the next burst of woodland and eventually you see fencing, a barrier and a road up ahead. The source of the **Beaulieu River** is nearby. (3 miles)

⑦ Turn right and walk along the road, passing **Fenwick Hospital**. Continue to the next junction, turn left, then immediately left to join a bridleway. Follow the track between laurel hedges and houses and in due course you join a road. Walk along to the junction and turn left. Return to the car park at **Swan Green**. (1 mile)

Date walk completed:

LEPE AND EXBURY

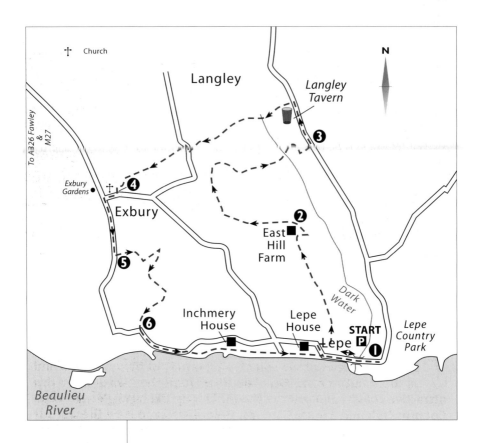

Distance:
8¹/₂ miles

Starting point:
The car park
(fee-paying) at
Lepe Country Park.
GR 455985

Map: OS Landranger 196 or OS Outdoor Leisure 22

How to get there: *From junction 2 of the M27, take the
A326 to Fawley, and then follow the signs for Lepe. The
car park overlooks the shore.*

THE LANGLEY TAVERN

*S*pectacular views of the Solent and pockets of tranquil woodland at the mouth of the Beaulieu River form the backdrop to this attractive coastal and country circuit. Among the highlights are Lepe Country Park and Exbury Gardens. Before setting out on the walk, it is advisable to check times of tides, which may affect the final foreshore stretch. Call Lepe Country Park on 02380 899108.

Built as a pub, the **Langley Tavern** in Langley, to the south of Blackfield, is a popular watering hole with walkers and sightseers. Its close proximity to Lepe Country Park, the sea, and the New Forest, makes it an obvious choice for food and drink, and the beer garden gets quite crowded on summer days. Snacks include baguettes, jacket potatoes, salads and sandwiches, while main meals range from gammon steak and lasagne to steak and ale pie and fish and chips. Food is served all day, every day and on Sunday there is a traditional roast. Real ales include Ringwood Best and a guest beer. Telephone: 02380 891402.

The Walk

Lepe Country Park is a fascinating setting in which to begin a walk. Characterised by shingle beaches, wild natural habitats, and clumps of pine trees, this stretch of the Hampshire coast remains hidden and undiscovered. To the west of the country park lie silent and eerie mudflats and marshland expanses at the mouth of the Beaulieu River. Have a look at the illustrated text boards which tell the fascinating story of Lepe's part in the preparations for D-Day in 1944.

① From the car park, follow the road towards **Exbury**, keeping the beach and foreshore over to your left. Stay on the road as it curves to the right by the **Millennium Beacon**, opened by the Lord Lieutenant of Hampshire in July 2000 and, when it bends left, turn right at a stile. Keep right in the field and follow the grassy track as it swings to the left, to a gateway. Make for the second gateway and keep to the left of a fence. Go straight ahead across fields and enter woodland. Drop down to a footbridge and turn right at the official diversion sign. Walk along to a gate, turn right, then immediately left, keeping to the left edge of the field. Make for **East Hill Farm** and join a concrete track. (1 ¹/₂ miles)

② Walk away from the farm and, when the track eventually bends sharp left, turn right to a galvanised gate and then immediately left, following a grassy path between trees, hedges and wooden fencing. Keep right in the next field and follow the path between fences. On reaching a junction with a track, turn right and enter coniferous woodland. When you emerge from the trees, avoid a track running down the slope to your left and continue through the woods. Soon you come to a fork. Keep left here and stay on the main path. Head down to the wonderfully named **Dark Water** and cross it via some round stepping stones. Go over a stile and footbridge and negotiate several more stiles before reaching the road. (2 miles)

③ Turn left and keep the **Langley Tavern** on the left and the **Langley Restaurant** on the right. Turn immediately left to join a bridleway running to the next road. Veer left at the fork, by the no through road sign, and pass **Homer Farm Lane**. Keep left at the next fork and follow the road as it dwindles to a track. Pass a bungalow called **Avalon** and keep ahead on a path running through woodland. Recross the **Dark Water** and follow the path as it

graduates to a track. Head up the slope to the road and turn right. Take a footpath on the left and cut between banks of bracken, thick in summer. Emerge from the trees into a field, swing left at a waymark and then veer right, after about 80 yards, to follow a track along the rear of some houses. Walk along to some bungalows and turn left at this point, heading for the road. (1 1/2 miles)

④ The remains of old petrol pumps – a reminder of when there was a filling station in the village – can be seen on the right. Turn right and head for a tall, distinctive water tower serving the Exbury estate. To visit

THE ROUTE NEAR EAST HILL FARM

St Katherine's church and **Exbury Gardens**, turn right; to continue the walk, turn left and follow **Inchmery Lane**. Head out of **Exbury** and, as the road begins to curve gradually to the right, turn left at a stile and waymark. Cross the field into woodland and to the right you can glimpse the ridge of the **Isle of Wight**.
($^3/_4$ mile)

Exbury Gardens, created by Lionel de Rothschild, a member of the famous banking family, are renowned for their outstanding collection of rhododendrons, magnolias and azaleas. There are superb woodland gardens and peaceful walks down to the banks of the Beaulieu River.

⑤ Enter the trees and follow the path across a footbridge. Make for the woodland edge and turn right here, following the footpath along the field boundary. Pass a waymark, avoid a track running into the wood and follow the field path as it runs outside the trees. Curve left in line with the field boundary and make for the hedge corner, where you'll find a waymark. Turn right along the field edge to a waymark and footbridge on the right, following the

LEPE

path through the tree-ringed pasture. Cross another footbridge and pass through a strip of woodland to reach a kissing gate. (³/₄ mile)

⑥ Turn left at the road, drop down the hill, and look for a footpath running parallel on the right. Follow the right of way along the foreshore and continue below **Inchmery House**. Pass **Lepe House**, join the road and cross over the **Dark Water** once more. Continue along the road and soon you reach the car park at **Lepe** where the walk began. (2 miles)

In the vicinity of Inchmery House there is evidence of concrete blocks and slipways associated with the building and launching of Mulberry harbours in the run-up to D-Day. Security was especially tight at this crucial time and special passes were needed to enter the area, residents of the nearby coastguard cottages had to get written permission even to go shopping. Lepe was a departure point for large numbers of troops, tanks and equipment. As D-Day approached, the stretch of water between Lepe and the Isle of Wight was tightly packed with landing craft and ships of every description. Elsewhere in the New Forest huge numbers of tanks and other vehicles gathered in the lanes and woodland tracks in readiness for the signal. At the end of the walk take a stroll east along the foreshore, beyond the car park, and you'll come to two four-legged structures, code-named 'Dolphin.' These were used as a jetty for the mooring of landing craft.

Date walk completed:

KING'S SOMBORNE AND THE CLARENDON WAY

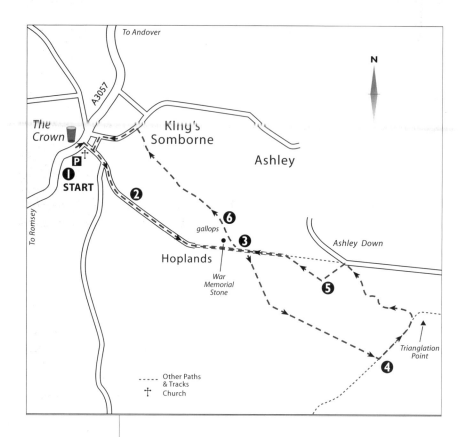

Distance:
7 miles

Starting point:
The car park off
the main street in
King's Somborne.
GR 358307

Map: OS Landranger 185 or OS Explorer 131

How to get there: *King's Somborne is on the A3057
between Andover and Romsey. You will find the car park
to the south of the war memorial and pub.*

APPROACHING KING'S SOMBORNE AT THE END OF THE WALK

S pectacular downland scenery forms the backdrop on this remote but varied walk in mid Hampshire. Swathes of downland and occasional bursts of woodland stretch to the horizon and at times you will experience few signs of life. As you will see from the map, the route is shaped like a figure of eight so it can easily be cut short if required. King's Somborne, where the walk begins, is one of Hampshire's larger villages. It was here that John of Gaunt, son of Edward III, had a deer park. On the outward leg of the walk there is a fascinating insight into a major incident in this area during the early months of the Second World War.

One of the oldest pubs in the area, the **Crown Inn**, is a 17th century thatched inn that, until only recently, was one of several hostelries in King's Somborne. Now it is the sole surviving pub in the village. Bar food ranges from sausage and mash and lamb cobbler to Somerset chicken and, on Sunday, a traditional roast. There are also various sandwiches, toasties and ploughman's lunches. No food is served on Tuesday evening. Real ales include Ringwood Best and Wadworth 6X. Telephone: 01794 388360.

 # The Walk

① From the car park in the centre of **King's Somborne**, turn right and follow the main street towards the school and war memorial. Turn right opposite the **Crown Inn** and follow **Church Road**. Ignore **Old Palace Farm**, a residential road on the right, and follow the road as gradually it climbs out of the village. Pass **Eldon Road** and continue up and over the brow of the hill. Keep left at the next junction. (¹/₂ mile)

② Avoid a right of way and continue along the lane as it runs virtually in a straight line, cutting between fields and hedgerows. Further on the road runs up a slope and through a pretty tunnel of trees, with glimpses over picturesque rolling countryside. Continue to **Hoplands**, an equestrian centre, and stay on the track as it picks its way between fields and trees. On the left along this stretch, sometimes slightly obscured by undergrowth, is a small memorial stone. (1¹/₂ miles)

The air campaign over southern England at the start of the Second World War was one of the biggest and most important military engagements in history. Looking at the sleepy village of King's Somborne and its peaceful, rural setting today, it is hard to believe that this area faced the horrors of war.

One day in the summer of 1940 fighter pilot Bob Doe picked out a lone Junkers 88 bomber in the skies above King's Somborne. Wasting no time in pinpointing his target, Doe launched a deadly attack on the plane and watched as it swiftly fell to earth. Later, he and his squadron leader drove to the spot where the plane came down – a field outside the village. On arrival, they discovered the wreckage guarded by Local Defence Volunteers who were there to deter souvenir hunters and excited children. The memorial stone in the verge reads: 'In memory of 4 unknown German airmen killed here – August 23, 1940'.

③ Beyond the stone is a junction with the **Clarendon Way**.

This 26-mile walk links Salisbury with Winchester and is named after a hunting lodge for Norman kings.

Continue ahead for a short distance and turn right, following a bridleway across fields and beside a line of trees. When the track bends left at a private sign, walk forward, avoiding the track running off to the right, and go straight over to join a path cutting between trees and bushes. Proceed through the wood, pass a tree-ringed field on the left and go over a cross-track. The path runs between trees and bracken for some time, at length crossing over a clear track to reach a T-junction. (1 $1/2$ miles)

④ Turn left at this point, keeping fields on the right. Follow the woodland path as it curves gently to the left, head for a barrier and turn sharp left to join the **Clarendon Way**. There are superb downland views here – vast fields stretch as far as the eye can see and the entire scene conveys a sense of complete isolation. At times on this walk it is as if you have suddenly stumbled upon a desolate, abandoned world

THE CROWN AND THE VILLAGE WAR MEMORIAL

PEACE AND QUIET ALONG THE WAY

almost completely devoid of human habitation. Follow the **Clarendon Way** beside woodland, descend to a track and cross over. Continue almost to the road. Don't join it. Instead, swing left here and follow the track up the slope. (1 mile)

⑤ Bend right by a gate and follow the fenced track as it undulates across the fields. Pass into some woodland, climb through a tunnel of trees and pass a crossroads with a right of way on the left. This junction represents the start of the return leg of the walk. Veer right just beyond it at the **Clarendon Way**

sign and cut through woodland to follow a lengthy section of path alongside gallops. (1 mile)

Over to the right across the fields is the little settlement of Ashley. This is where the fondly remembered Scottish actor James Roberston Justice lived in rural seclusion. He appeared in many British films during his long career, mainly in character roles, but Robertson Justice's most famous part was that of Sir Lancelot Spratt in the 'Doctor' comedy films of the 1950s and 60s. With his bulky frame and bellowing voice, he was instantly recognisable as the irascible surgeon. As well as acting, Robertson Justice turned his hand to many jobs over the years. He was also Rector of the University of Edinburgh and inventor of the rocket propelled net method of catching wildfowl for marking. James Robertson Justice died in 1975, two weeks after his 70th birthday.

⑥ When the gallops eventually sweep left, continue straight on along the **Clarendon Way**. Cross several stiles and keep to the field boundary. Curve right and follow the way down to the road. Turn left at this point and head for the centre of **King's Somborne**. Bend left, pass the village post office and go right at the T-junction. Pass the church and return to the car park where the walk began. (1¹/₂ miles)

Date walk completed:

WHERWELL, HAREWOOD FOREST AND THE RIVER TEST

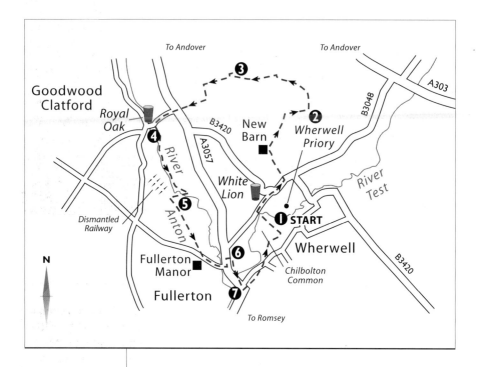

Distance:
10½ miles

Starting point:
Wherwell village
centre.
GR 388407

Map: OS Landranger 185 or Explorer 131

How to get there: *Wherwell is on the B3420 just off the A3057 Andover to Romsey road. There is room to park in the High Street.*

THE RIVER TEST AT WHERWELL

*R*oyal scandal is nothing new but today's lurid headlines pale into insignificance alongside the dark deeds of a scheming 10th century king and queen. Picture the distant past and discover what took place amid the peace and seclusion of Harewood Forest as you make your way through the trees to Goodworth Clatford and on to a picturesque reach of the River Anton where it meets the Test. Though hard to spot, you may be lucky enough to see a kingfisher as you follow a delightfully pretty stretch of the Test Way across Chilbolton Common and back into Wherwell.

From the outside the **Royal Oak** in Goodworth Clatford looks rather like a modern detached family home. Inside, it couldn't be more different. The bars are large and spacious, wood panelling abounds and there is even some stained glass. You can choose from a wide selection of dishes listed on blackboards above and around the bar, among them various steaks, scampi, burger and chips, chicken and mushroom pie, sausage and mash, ham, egg and chips and plenty more. There is always a range of baguettes, including bacon, lettuce and tomato, cheddar and ham. Ringwood Best, Flowers Original and Fuller's London Pride are some of the real ales available. The beer garden is popular on fine days. The Royal Oak keeps traditional hours and is open 7 days a week. Telephone: 01264 324105.

The Walk

① Make for the village war memorial in **Wherwell**. Keep **Church Street** on your right and walk along the road, passing lines of thatched, timber-framed cottages on the right. On the left is a house with a large picture window. Pass the entrance to **Wherwell Priory**, then some more thatched cottages and swing left by the **Old Smithy**. Following the **Test Way**, pass the remains of a disused railway almost immediately and then continue to climb steadily, the route coinciding now with a sunken path. Descend to a track, then cross over and keep to the right of some barns and a single-storey dwelling. This is **New Barn**. Start climbing again and follow the path between fields and fences. Skirt woodland, following the southern boundary of **Harewood Forest**, and look out for pheasants as they skurry through the undergrowth on hearing your approach. Pass a path on the left and avoid one on the right. Keep ahead for about 150 yards to some isolated barns and outbuildings. (1½ miles)

More than one thousand years ago Harewood Forest was the setting for a Machiavellian scheme of murder by royal command. North of the A303, off the route of this walk and heavily obscured by trees, is a tall 19th century monument known as 'Dead Man's Plack'. This forgotten landmark recalls the murder of Earl Aetholwold by Saxon King Edgar in the forest in AD 965. Apparently eager to meet Elfrida, daughter of a duke and a renowned beauty, Edgar despatched one of his courtiers, Earl Aetholwold, to assess her suitability as a bride. Not surprisingly, the earl was smitten by her charm and beauty and he promptly married her himself. Suspecting something of the sort might have taken place, Edgar visited Elfrida in person at Wherwell. On learning what had happened and realising she had been denied the opportunity to become queen, Elfrida turned her remarkable charms fully towards King Edgar and together the pair plotted to kill Aetholwold. Edgar arranged a hunting trip for the two of them in Harewood Forest. There, the king stabbed him to death, thus enabling Elfrida to become his queen. When he died, Edgar was succeeded to the throne by his eldest son Edward,

Elfrida's stepson. However, the queen was anxious to see her own son Ethelred (the Unready) become king and soon dark forces within the royal family were at work once more. Elfrida had Edward stabbed to death at Corfe Castle in AD 978. Her own son then succeeded to the throne. The queen later lived a life of quiet seclusion at Wherwell Priory, no doubt haunted by her conscience. She died in 1002.

② Turn left immediately beyond the buildings and follow the track downhill through the trees and then round to the right at the bottom. Go

THE ROYAL OAK AT GOODWORTH CLATFORD

straight over at a major junction and keep on the concrete track through the forest. Go left at a fork and make for a T-junction in the depths of the woodland. Surrounding you on this stretch of the walk are conifers and silver birch trees – among other species. Opposite is a cistern that was quite possibly used as a water tank when the forest was transformed into an ammunition depot during the Second World War. Turn left and follow the straight track to two dilapidated Nissen huts – two more reminders of recent conflict. They are now used for storing chicken coops and the like. Continue ahead, following the path through a belt of woodland. On reaching a gate, turn left in the field and follow the perimeter to the end of the wire fence. (1¹/₂ miles)

③ Turn left at the waymark, then keep the fencing on your left and make for a wide gap in the trees. Pass through the gap and keep right along the field boundary. Eventually you reach a track. Turn left here and pass under power lines. Go up the slope between hedges and take a path on the right to pass between the fairways of a golf course. On reaching the road, cross over into **Church Lane** and head for **Goodworth Clatford**, passing **St Peter's Close**. Walking through the village, pass **Goodworth Lodge** and cross the **River Anton**. Pass an attractive map of the area prepared by the Parish Council and

turn right at the next junction for the **Royal Oak**. (2 miles)

④ Retrace your steps to the **River Anton** and turn right at a sign for **Anton Cottage**. Following the bridleway, pass through a wrought iron kissing gate and keep to the right of the pumping station. Cut between trees and hedges and stay on the path as it climbs above the river. The path then runs through woodland and across fields, passing to the right of a sewage treatment plant. Continue until you reach a path running off to the right. Take this and cross the **Anton** at the footbridge. Swing right in the watermeadow, alongside the river. When it bends right, go straight on across the fields and follow the track to the dismantled railway. (1¹/₂ miles)

⑤ Turn left and walk along to a galvanised gate. Veer right here, taking the grassy track up the hillside and into the next field. Continue ahead and look out for a radio telescope ahead in the distance. Make for the road opposite **Fullerton Manor** and turn left. Note the village sign for **Fullerton**. Pass a pretty thatched cottage on the left and a mill on the right. Less than a mile downstream from here the **Anton** meets the **Test**. (1¹/₂ miles)

⑥ On reaching the main road, turn left and cross the former railway. Go down to the sign for **Cottonworth** and swing right to join a footpath by a letterbox. Follow the tarmac lane between houses and pass **Fullerton's old station buildings**. The garden is the site of the old station and the remains of the trackbed and the platforms can still be seen.

This was originally the meeting point of two railways – the London to Salisbury line and the Andover to Southampton line. The former opened in 1885 and was well loved by Queen Victoria, who used this route when travelling to Osborne House on the Isle of Wight.

Pass a sign for the **Test Way Countryside Service** and keep ahead through the trees. Soon the **River Test** edges into view – completing a classic picture of the English countryside. The sturdy sleepers here recall the great age of railway travel when the leviathans of steam sped along this twin-track line. As you approach the road bridge, turn left and follow the wall to the road. ($^1/_2$ mile)

⑦ Cross over and take some steps up the hillside. At the top keep a seat on the right and follow the path parallel to the road. At length it descends gradually to reach **West Down car park**. Turn left for several paces along the road, then go right at the sign for the **Test Way**. Follow the path across a drive and continue between wooden panel fencing and trees to enter the **Memorial Playing Fields** via a kissing gate. Cross the playing fields to a track, follow it to the left of a thatched cottage and turn left just before a cattle-grid. Stay with the **Test Way** across 48-acre **Chilbolton Common**, cross the **Test** and turn right at the road. Return to the centre of **Wherwell**, passing the White Lion pub. (2 miles)

Date walk completed:
23.9.06

HURSTBOURNE TARRANT AND UPTON

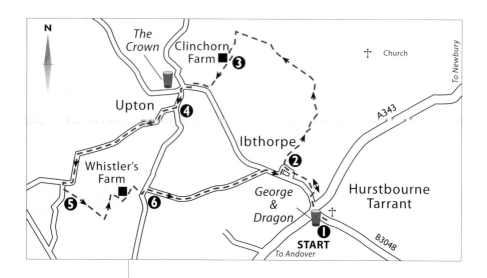

Distance:
10 miles

Starting point:
The free car park
in Hurstbourne
Tarrant.
GR 385527

Map: OS Landranger 185 or Explorer 131

How to get there: *Follow the A343 road between Andover and Newbury and on reaching Hurstbourne Tarrant take the turning at the side of the George and Dragon. The entrance to the car park is on the right, opposite the church.*

THE CROWN AT UPTON

*T*hroughout this circuit the scenery typifies Hampshire at its glorious best. The north of the county is characterised by dramatically rolling hills and picturesque valleys – perfect for exploring on foot. Beyond the village of Hurstbourne Tarrant the walk makes for remote country straddling the Wiltshire and Berkshire border before heading south-west to the village of Upton and on to Rushmore Down.

The **Crown Inn** at Upton is a well established pub in this corner of Hampshire. It has a quaint exterior and cottagey appearance that make it blend easily into the village. Recently refurbished and extended, it is as shiny as a new pin inside, as well as very roomy. The restaurant is ideal for small parties of around ten, while the conservatory can seat 20 people on one large table. There is also a barn, suitable for parties of up to 12. The bar menu usually offers the likes of steak and kidney pie, battered cod and chips and chilli beef and rice. The set restaurant menu might include breast of chicken with prawn and sherry sauce and poached salmon with lemon and cracked black pepper glaze. There is also a set roast menu. Real ales include Fuller's London Pride and Ringwood Best. The Crown is open everyday, both lunchtime and in the evening. At the back is a popular beer garden. Telephone: 01264 736265

 The Walk

A long main street of pretty thatched cottages with a 17th century coaching inn at the foot of a steep hill create an atmosphere of charm and genteel beauty at the heart of the Hampshire countryside, blighted only by the scar of a busy main road. This is Hurstbourne Tarrant, one of the county's loveliest villages, sitting pretty in a lush, steep-sided valley between the towns of Newbury and Andover. The setting is also the meeting point for two of Hampshire's smaller, lesser-known waterways – the Bourne rivulet and the River Swift. However, there is more to Hurstbourne Tarrant than a casual stroll might reveal.

The 'Tarrant' comes from the Dorset village of Tarrant Crawford, whose nuns owned land here, but it was the writer William Cobbett who helped to lift its profile, describing the place in glowing prose in his 'Rural Rides', a social record of rural life and agricultural hardship. Hurstbourne Tarrant was Cobbett's favourite village – 'a sight worth going many miles to see,' he claimed. He was just as complimentary about the spectacular surrounding countryside that forms the backdrop for this very attractive and enjoyable walk. 'To stand upon any of the hills and look around you, you almost think you see the ups and downs of sea in a heavy swell ... The undulations are endless, and the great variety in the ... little hills has a very delightful effect.'

Dominating the scene as the eastern end of Hurstbourne Tarrant is the village church, with its flint façade, squat design and weather-boarded bell turret topped by a spire. St Peter's has a medieval wall painting depicting the legend of the three living kings and the three dead kings. According to some sources, three kings meet three skeletons while out hunting, reminding them of their own mortality. The main part of the church dates from the late 12th and early 13th centuries.

① From the village car park follow the road through **Hurstbourne Tarrant** to the A343. Make for the **George and Dragon** and on the wall you can see a blue plaque commemorating the life of the English actor-manager Sir Donald Wolfit (1902–68) who lived locally. Cross over with care and take the road signposted to **Upton** and **Ibthorpe**. Continue towards the outer edge of **Hurstbourne Tarrant** and take the path to the right of the village hall, passing through a wrought iron kissing gate. Almost at once you reach a fork. Veer left here, following the **Test Way**. Keep left along the field edge, the delightful little **Swift** trickling almost unseen just a few yards

ROLLING COUNTRYSIDE NEAR UPTON

away. Cross the next field and pass through several gates to arrive at a track. Turn left opposite a thatched barn and continue round to the right to a junction with a lane. Opposite is **Elm Cottage**. Turn right here and follow the lane alongside pretty thatched cottages, bending left at the sign for the **Test Way**. On reaching the next junction, opposite a thatched cottage, turn right. (1 mile)

② Head towards some corrugated farm outbuildings and keep on the **Test Way**, following the arrows and waymarks. Go up a gentle slope between hedgerows and when you reach a junction with a triangular patch of grass, keep left. Almost immediately the track swings to the right. On the right is a barn, rather reminiscent of a wartime Nissen hut. Look for a **Test Way** sign here. Now the track curves to the left and along this stretch are good views back down towards the **Bourne valley** and across to the more rugged, rolling country straddling the Hampshire/Wiltshire/Berkshire border. Keep on the track, passing pylons, and over to the right are extensive afforested slopes. Soon the route ahead becomes enclosed by trees and bushes. Avoid a turning on the left and when you reach a major intersection of tracks, with pylons on the right, turn left and descend gradually into the valley. (2 miles)

③ Pass the remains of derelict farm outbuildings – **Clinchorn Farm** – and follow the undulating track as it reveals very pleasant views over a rolling Hampshire landscape. Drop down steeply at one point and below you is **Upton**. On reaching the village, turn right at the road and walk along to the **Old Post Office**. Keep ahead to the **Crown**, then retrace your steps to the turning for **Wildhern** and **Andover**. Pass the **Old School House** and **School Hill Cottages** and continue beyond the 30-mile derestriction sign. As the road swings left, turn right to follow a track. (1³/₄ miles)

④ Pass between trees and beside a barn and when the track bends left by a 'private' sign towards more outbuildings, go straight on uphill. It is quite a pull up here, but the surroundings more than compensate for the exertion. This is a delightfully rural enclave, with few signs of civilisation. Keep to the right of a gate and 'private' sign and continue climbing quite steeply. Walk ahead on the higher ground, passing through extensive woodland, and at length the path bends sharp left. Stay on it until you reach a lane and turn left at this point, keeping trees on your left. (1³/₄ miles)

⑤ Very soon you reach a galvanised gate on the left. Swing left and follow the track through the belt of woodland. There are fields either side and good views to the right. When you reach a tarmac lane on a bend, with a cattle-grid on the right, turn left and pass a footpath sign on the left. The lane bends sharp right and cuts between trees and hedges. On reaching **Whistler's Farm**, follow the enclosed path to the right of it, passing between trees and banks of undergrowth. The path is not well used and can be a little difficult to negotiate in places. At the end of this section, turn right in front of a wire fence and follow the track down to the road. (1¼ miles)

⑥ Turn left and walk down to a turning on the right (**Locke's Drove**). Follow the tarmac lane and pass a bungalow with shutters on the left. Pass a transmitter and various dilapidated outbuildings and follow the drove road all the way to the road. Turn right and walk along to **Ibthorpe House**.

Ibthorpe House is a striking Georgian building of chequered brick. Jane Austen often stayed here with her friends, the Lloyds, and it is known that she attended church services at Hurstbourne Tarrant.

Swing left here and when you reach a fork, keep right and now retrace your steps back to the car park at **Hurstbourne Tarrant**. (2½ miles)

Date walk completed:

BEACON HILL AND BURGHCLERE

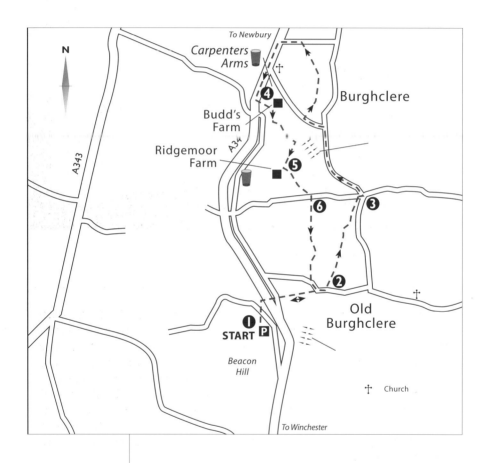

Distance:
7³/₄ miles

Starting point:
Beacon Hill car
park. GR 463575

Map: OS Landranger 174 or Explorer 144 and 158

How to get there: *Beacon Hill car park is just off the
A34 to the south of Newbury.*

THE CARPENTERS ARMS AT BURGHCLERE

*T*his spectacular walk combines fine downland views with sheltered tracks and peaceful woodland paths. The route starts at the foot of Beacon Hill, a much-loved beauty spot on the Hampshire/Berkshire border, and then makes for Burghclere and the Sandham Memorial Chapel, which is famous for its superb murals by Stanley Spencer, immensely moving and probably his finest work. If you want to extend the walk, a climb to the top of Beacon Hill – it rises to 858 ft – is well worthwhile. From the top there is a magnificent panoramic view of the Kennet valley to the north and the Test valley to the south.

A popular pub in this corner of North Hampshire, the **Carpenters Arms** in Burghclere has a refined, almost rarefied atmosphere. The bar area has casement windows, comfortable sofas, tables and chairs, log fires in winter, attractive paintings and a selection of daily newspapers. Relaxed, civilised surroundings indeed. As well as a varied range of meals, there is a good choice of baguettes and sandwiches with fillings such as sausage and mustard, or ham and asparagus. The pub has a part timbered bar and a brick conservatory restaurant. Real ales include Arkells 3B. Telephone. 01635 278231.

 The Walk

One of North Hampshire's most prominent landmarks, Beacon Hill is an Iron Age hill fort defended by a bank, ditch and counterscarp bank. Its single entrance faces the natural approach along a ridge and is protected by extra banks. The sites of about 20 round huts can be traced within the defences. If you are feeling energetic and adventurous, you might like to climb to the top of the hill. I have gone up on several occasions and though it's hard work the effort is well worth it for the views alone. Surprisingly, you'll find a solitary grave on the top – that of the 5th Earl of Carnarvon, who expressed a desire to be buried up here overlooking his beloved home, Highclere Castle. Born at Highclere in 1866, the Earl became interested in archaeology when at Cambridge and for 16 years he and Howard Carter

conducted fieldwork and excavations in Egypt. Their most famous discovery came in November 1922 – Tutankhamun's tomb.

① From the car park at **Beacon Hill** cross the A34 via the bridge and look for a footpath on the far side of the road. Skirt the field to **Old Burghclere church**, pass the entrance to **Burghclere Manor** and on reaching the road on a bend, go straight on. (³/₄ mile)

Interestingly, the old signpost here still points to Burghclere station to the right, though it closed in the mid 1960s, a casualty of the Beeching axe. The line ran from Didcot to Southampton and was in continuous service for almost 80 years.

② Cross the dismantled railway and turn immediately left to join a footpath. Keep the trees on your left and over to the right you can see the ridge of **Watership Down**. Enter woodland in the field corner, keep the old trackbed parallel on the left and follow a broad grassy ride through the woods. With its clear air and stands of fir trees, this sheltered stretch of the walk is perhaps more reminiscent of Scotland or Northumberland than Hampshire. Maintain the same direction through the wood and look out for deer skipping between the trees in the distance, no doubt startled by your footsteps. Pheasants, too, inhabit these surroundings. Breaking cover from the wood, veer right in line with a ditch and make for a stile across the field. Cross it and keep left alongside a hedge. Pass through a gap into the next elongated field and make for a stile up ahead. (1 mile)

③ Join the road and walk ahead, passing a byway. Keep left at the junction for **Burghclere** and follow the lane between hedgerows. Avoid a path and pass several farms and some brick cottages before turning left into **Spring Lane**. Pass **Pax Cottage** and continue to the point where a footpath crosses the road. Turn right through a galvanised gate and skirt the field to a footbridge. Follow the path through woodland to the next field and continue ahead. Cross into the next field and

THE NATIONAL TRUST'S SANDHAM MEMORIAL CHAPEL

head for the road. Turn left to **Burghclere church** and keep left at the junction. Walk through the village as far as the **Sandham Memorial Chapel**. (2^1/$_2$ miles)

The chapel was built in 1926-27 by Mr and Mrs J.L. Behrend who commissioned it as a war memorial and a specific monument to H.W. Sandham, who died in 1919 from an illness contracted during the First World War in Macedonia. The architect was Lionel Pearson and Stanley Spencer was responsible for the hugely impressive and ambitious murals, which took six years to complete and are reputed to be the most important series of decorative paintings produced in England this century. The images represent scenes from the Great War in which Spencer served as an orderly in a military hospital. The chapel is in the care of the National Trust and is open to the public between April and October.

④ Continue along the road to the **Carpenters Arms** and beyond it pass alongside modern houses and period cottages. Look for **Parsons Corner**, an old chapel, and as the road curves right by the speed derestriction sign turn left to join a no through road. Drop down the hill, pass a farm and turn right at a footpath sign. Cut between wooden and wire fences and cross two stiles.

Go straight ahead across the field, keeping to the right of **Budd's Farm**. Make for two stiles in the boundary ahead and follow the path with the outbuildings still on your left. Head for a stile by a galvanised gate, swing right and follow the tree-lined path between fields. At the next stile keep right in the field and make your way down to the bottom corner. Cross a stile on the right and follow the woodland path, keeping to its right-hand edge. Cross a section of boardwalk through the wood and beyond the next stile take the field path up the slope to a stile leading out to a lane. (^{3}/$_4$ mile)

⑤ Turn left, pass some timber-built semi-detached houses and continue on the single-track lane as it snakes through the countryside. Pass **Clere House** and **Ridgemoor Cottage** and keep ahead, avoiding a path on the right by a white gate. Pass between the outbuildings and barns of **Ridgemoor Farm**, part of the **Sydmonton Court Estate**, and continue on what is now a gravel track. Follow the waymarked byway and further on it starts to climb, running beneath the branches of trees at this stage. (^{3}/$_4$ mile)

⑥ Go straight on at a crossroads and follow the track as it descends steeply. In a gateway on the right the green bulk of **Beacon Hill** dominates the scene. Begin a gentle climb and further on the buildings of **Manor Farm** edge into view. At the road keep left, with the outbuildings on the right. Turn right at the bend in **Old Burghclere**, pass **Burghclere Manor** and go through a kissing gate to reach the church. Retrace your steps across the field and return to the car park at the foot of **Beacon Hill**. (2 miles)

Date walk completed:

KINGSCLERE AND WATERSHIP DOWN

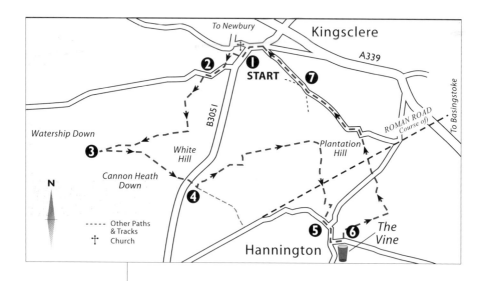

Distance:
11¼ miles

Starting point:
The free car park off Anchor Road in Kingsclere.
GR 525585

Map: OS Landranger 174 or Explorer 144

How to get there: *Kingsclere is on the A339 midway between Newbury and Basingstoke. Turn into Anchor Road by the church, in the village centre.*

THE VINE AT HANNINGTON

ome of the south of England's most dramatic downland scenery
forms the backdrop to this magnificent walk. From Kingsclere,
famous for its horse-racing connections, the route makes for the
edge of Watership Down, the isolated domain of those now
legendary rabbits, before heading for the peaceful village of
Hannington, with its pretty green and church.

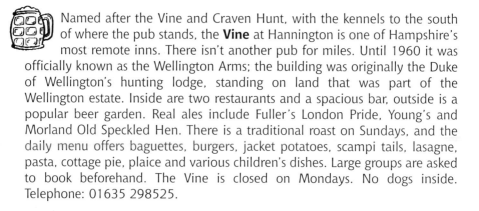

Named after the Vine and Craven Hunt, with the kennels to the south of where the pub stands, the **Vine** at Hannington is one of Hampshire's most remote inns. There isn't another pub for miles. Until 1960 it was officially known as the Wellington Arms; the building was originally the Duke of Wellington's hunting lodge, standing on land that was part of the Wellington estate. Inside are two restaurants and a spacious bar, outside is a popular beer garden. Real ales include Fuller's London Pride, Young's and Morland Old Speckled Hen. There is a traditional roast on Sundays, and the daily menu offers baguettes, burgers, jacket potatoes, scampi tails, lasagne, pasta, cottage pie, plaice and various children's dishes. Large groups are asked to book beforehand. The Vine is closed on Mondays. No dogs inside. Telephone: 01635 298525.

The Walk

The village of Kingsclere dates back to Saxon times, although there were people residing here before then. The West Saxons were not ones for city life and they considered the downland area in which the village is situated a perfect spot for a settlement. The site offered a constant supply of water and plentiful pasture for the animals. The surrounding woodland would have provided timber for building and fuel. Kingsclere was Klere in the 9th century, Cleare or Clera in the 10th century, and Clere in the 11th. By the 13th century, as a result of visits by several kings to nearby Freemantle, where Henry II built a royal hunting lodge, it had become known as Kyngescler. During the Civil War, King Charles I spent the night of 21 October 1644 at Frobury Manor, just to the north-west of the village.

St Mary's church in Kingsclere is Norman, though it was heavily restored in 1848-49. The north doorway is original. The chapel, on the south side, contains splendid alabaster monuments to Sir Henry Kingsmill and his wife Lady Bridget. Sir Henry is portrayed in the armour of Charles Ist's reign and lies on a plaited rush mattress, while his wife is fashioned in the clothes of a later period. She rests beside her husband in flowing garments with a shawl covering her hair. In her hand she holds a book and a handkerchief.

① Make for the churchyard entrance and take the tarmac path on the far side. Pass a pond on the right and turn right by a wooden panel fence. Cross several bridges and turn left.

Follow a path between fences to a wrought iron kissing gate, which leads out to the road. Turn left and continue along the road out of **Kingsclere**. Ahead the landscape is dominated by the ridge of **Watership Down**. ($^1/_2$ mile)

② Keep going until you reach a gate and opening on the left. Skirt the field along a broad grassy path until you reach a gap in the boundary. Follow the path between fields, heading towards the grassy slopes of **Watership Down** and **Cannon Heath Down**. On reaching a junction with a clear track, turn right and head in a westerly direction.

Make for a line of trees at right-angles to the track and turn left to join a path running up through a belt of woodland to a stile. Climbing dramatically now, the path heads diagonally right across the slopes of the escarpment – this section of the walk conveys a real sense of adventure. Keep the fence on the left and make for a stile. Go slightly left, cross the all-weather gallops and go diagonally across the grass towards bushes. This is the edge of **Watership Down**. (2 miles)

If you have the time and the energy, you might like to extend the walk at this point by following

BREEZY CANNON HEATH DOWN

the track in a westerly direction. This allows you to explore more of this isolated downland country. A visit to Watership Down, only a few minutes' walk away, takes you to what is surely one of the world's best-known literary landmarks, though you won't find any signs of commercialisation here. Signposted walks and a visitor centre are definitely not part of the attractions.

It was Richard Adams, a civil servant with the Department of the Environment, who chose this lonely hillside as the setting for his enchanting story of rabbit folk. Published in 1972, the book quickly became a bestseller and it remains a popular favourite with both children and adults to this day. Born in 1920, Adams made his home at nearby Whitchurch so it seemed logical to use the surrounding downland country as the story's backdrop. As someone who has lived on the Hampshire/Berkshire border for many years, I like to try and seek out the locations in the book, blending reality with fantasy and savouring the thrill of recreating the rabbits' journey in search of a new home when their ancient warren is threatened with destruction.

③ To continue the circular walk, follow the chalk track east, the television **mast** at **Hannington**

acting as a useful directional landmark. The route coincides at this point with the **Wayfarer's Walk**, following it all the way to the B3051 road at **White Hill**. (1¼ miles)

Along the way the route crosses the top of Cannon Heath Down. The name comes from the connection with the canons of Rouen in France. Henry I granted the manor of Kingsclere to the canons of the church of St Mary at Rouen. They held it virtually uninterrupted until 1335 and its revenue helped finance the building of Rouen Cathedral.

④ Cross the road and veer right by the entrance to the car park, staying on the route of the **Wayfarer's Walk**. Cut between trees and undergrowth until you come to a stile and gate on the left. Cross over and skirt the field edge, keeping the fence on the right. Make for the **mast** and look for a double stile in the corner. Cross over, then maintain the field boundary on the right and head for a galvanised gate and stile. Don't cross it; instead, turn left and follow the perimeter fence to the corner. Keep ahead down the pasture to a stile and footpath sign. Turn right and follow the path along the woodland edge. Eventually the path crosses an open field to reach a bridle track. Turn right here and go straight ahead at a junction of tracks. Cross the line of the **Portway**, clearly identified on maps but not seen on the ground.

The Romans began building roads following the invasion of AD 43, and the network gradually covered all of Roman Britain. Initially, the roads were constructed to meet military needs, but eventually they became major trade and communications routes, helping and boosting the local economy. The Portway is a typical example of a Roman road, stretching from Calleva, otherwise known as Silchester, to Old Sarum.

Follow the track to the left, then the right, and make for a gate in the field corner. (2¹/₂ miles)

⑤ Turn left and follow the road to the junction, veering right for the village of **Hannington**. On reaching the spacious village green, keep ahead for a short distance to reach the **Vine**. Retrace your steps to the green and church and take the turning on the right. Walk along to

Bertha's Cottage and swing left by **Michael's Field**. (1 mile)

⑥ Follow the track to a bridleway sign and turn right. Take the obvious track across the fields to the next junction, turn left and follow the bridleway down to a road. Cross over and keep ahead on the bridleway, recrossing the **Portway**. Ascend to a junction, veer right towards **Plantation Hill** and follow the track towards houses and farm outbuildings. Keep ahead on a tarmac road and when it curves right, go straight on down a very pleasant green lane, offering memorable views up towards **White Hill** and the **Hannington mast**. Pass a bridleway leading off sharp left and keep right at the fork just beyond. (3 miles)

⑦ Join a tarmac path cutting between houses on the edge of **Kingsclere** and follow it down to the main road. Turn left and walk down **George Street**. Take a leisurely stroll through the village before returning to the car park. (1 mile)

Date walk completed:

EVERSLEY CHURCH AND BRAMSHILL FOREST

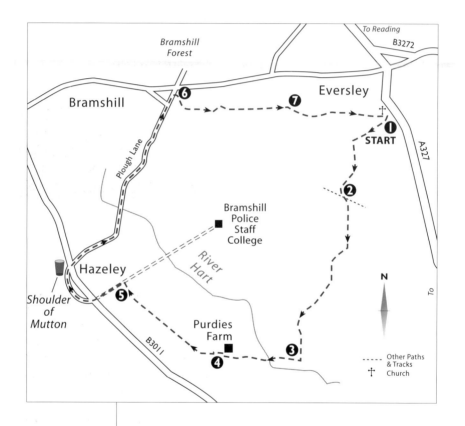

Distance:
8³/₄ miles

Starting point:
Eversley church.
GR 778608

Map: OS Landranger 175 or OS Explorer 144 and 159

How to get there: *Eversley village is on the A327, just inside the county boundary. Approaching from the M3, leave at junction 4a and take the A327 north towards Reading. Turn off westwards at Eversley church and park in the vicinity of the entrance.*

THE SHOULDER OF MUTTON AT HAZELEY

*I*f you don't know it and have never been there, Bramshill Forest comes as something of a surprise. Vast and slightly mysterious, it brings to mind, in places, one of those 1960s Cold War thrillers that are shown on television from time to time. Once inside it, you could easily be forgiven for thinking that a car carrying sinister henchman might appear at any moment. Then, perhaps rather predictably, Michael Caine emerges from the trees, wearing dark-rimmed glasses and a mac. I doubt very much this sprawling wooded landscape would be familiar to the likes of Len Deighton or John le Carré but here and there Bramshill Forest does look as if it comes straight from the pages of spy fiction. It has a strange, almost unsettling atmosphere.

The delightful **Shoulder of Mutton** pub at Hazeley dates back to the 1830s. Inside, the atmosphere and surroundings are cosy and charming, with low beams and wintertime log fires adding to the appeal. The menu is wide-ranging and extensive and among the dishes are ham, egg and chips, liver and bacon casserole, lasagne and curry. Lighter fare includes filled rolls and jacket potatoes. Outside is a large garden that is very popular in summer. Real ales include Courage Best and Wadworth 6X. Telephone: 0118 932 6272.

 *The Walk*

Before starting the walk have a look at the curious sarsen stone hidden beneath a trap door inside Eversley church. Discovered in 1940, it may well be part of the foundations of a heathen place of worship. The Victorian author Charles Kingsley (see Walk 12), who wrote the children's classic 'The Water Babies', was rector here for many years and is buried alongside his wife Fanny near the main door. Kingsley also wrote novels – among them 'Hereward the Wake' – as well as

EVERSLEY CHURCH

various songs and ballads. A committed Christian Socialist, he was appointed a canon of Westminster and chaplain to Queen Victoria. Above Kingsley's grave is a striking white marble cross with the words 'God is love' inscribed on it. Look for the Irish yews, planted by Kingsley, lining the path from the lychgate.

① With **Eversley church** on your right, follow the **Three Castles Path**, linking Winchester, Odiham and Windsor, down to some gates. Turn left at this point and skirt the woodland. Keep left at the fork and make for a broad junction of tracks. (1 mile)

② Go straight over and continue ahead at the next junction. Follow the wide track to another spacious intersection, veer half-right here and walk down to a fork. Keep left and cross over a track. At this stage the path becomes a track providing access to a number of buildings and industrial units. (1½ miles)

③ At the point where the track bends left, turn right over a stile into a paddock. Head for a galvanised gate and cross to several stiles and a footbridge. Keep on the path ahead,

THE ENTRANCE TO BRAMSHILL HOUSE

looking for a gap and stile on the left. Follow the fenced path towards woodland, cross the **River Hart** via two footbridges and go right, walking along the duckboard sections to the next wood. Climb between banks of vegetation, which includes bracken in the summer months, and turn right at the drive. ($^3/_4$ mile)

④ Swing left after a few paces in front of **Purdies Farm** and follow the path along the edge of a wood. Pass some kennels and continue on the track to a right-hand bend by a lodge. Cross the stile at this point and keep to the right of a lake. Make for another stile and go ahead through the trees. The outline of **Bramshill Police Staff College** is visible now over to the right. Join a drive, keep left and head for the imposing college entrance. (1 mile)

⑤ Turn left here and follow the drive to the road. Turn right, cross over and take the lane on the left, heading for the **Shoulder of Mutton** pub. With your back to the building, turn left to the main road and cross over into **Plough Lane**. Follow it for some time – usually the traffic is quite light along here. Eventually you reach a turning for **Heckfield** on the left and an entrance to **Bramshill College** on the right. (2 miles)

Bramshill House is a splendid Jacobean pile – one of the finest anywhere in the country. Built in 1612 by Lord Zouche, the house is associated with the legend of the mistletoe bough chest. A young bride, tired of the formal reception following her wedding ceremony, plays hide and seek, excitedly climbing into a chest she has found in some distant corner of the house. Tragically, the lid snaps shut and she is trapped, her screams for help unheeded. Years later the bride's skeleton is discovered, wrapped in her wedding dress.

The plight of the young girl forms the basis for a Victorian ballad, 'The Mistletoe Bough', written by T.H. Bayly in 1828 and set to music by the conductor Sir Henry Bishop. It is claimed the ballad is based on a true story and three historic houses in Hampshire are believed by some to be possible candidates as locations for the tragic events retold in Bayly's ballad – one of them being Bramshill. In the hall here is a splendid Italian chest, richly inlaid with figures in 16th century dress and said to be the genuine bough chest in which the girl perished. The chest is the subject of a covenant which dictates that it will always stay at Bramshill.

⑥ Pass over the junction and look for a path on the right. Follow the waymarked **Welsh Drive** bridleway to a junction in front of a fence and turn right. Keep alongside the fence to the corner, where you turn left, then right. At this stage there are lakes either side of the path. Merge with another path, then turn left to follow a narrow, tree-shaded path. On reaching a broad track, turn right and pass alongside clumps of pine trees to reach another **Welsh Drive** sign. Turn sharp left about 60 yards before a fingerpost and follow the colour-coded waymarks through the pine trees and bracken, turning right at a wide track. When the track swings right, keep ahead, with pine trees on your right. (1¹/₂ miles)

⑦ Go straight ahead at the next waymark and cross a track to follow a path which runs just inside the wood. Open fields are seen on the left along here. Follow the path down to the woodland corner, pass through a kissing gate and head straight on. When the path swings left, go ahead through another kissing gate. Continue ahead in the field and make for a narrow path in the corner. Follow it to a gate and footbridge and enter **Eversley churchyard**. Cut through it to the parking area at the start of the walk. (1¹/₂ miles)

Date walk completed:

ODIHAM AND THE BASINGSTOKE CANAL

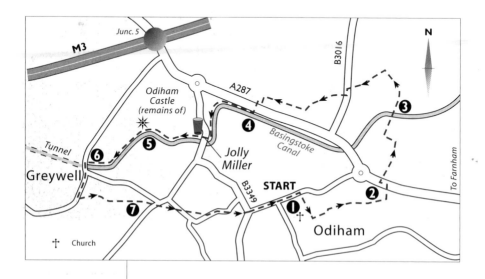

Distance:
7¹/₂ miles

Starting point:
Odiham High
Street.
GR 741511

Map: OS Landranger 186 or Explorer 144

How to get there: *Odiham is about 6 miles east of Basingstoke near junction 5 of the M3 and is just off the A287. There is parking in the town.*

THE JOLLY MILLER AT NORTH WARNBOROUGH

*O*diham is located in one of the more densely populated corners of Hampshire. But don't let that put you off. Outside the town are tracts of pretty countryside bisected by the delightful Basingstoke Canal, one of the south's most popular waterways. This very varied walk starts in Odiham and then crosses farmland to follow the canal towpath. In due course you reach the remains of King John's Castle, located by the water. Only the octagonal keep survives and in a certain light in the depths of winter, the castle ruin is deliciously eerie, the long shadows, the crumbling walls and the glow of the setting sun creating a magical atmosphere. You half expect the figure of King John to materialise before you. From the Greywell Tunnel on the canal the route returns to Odiham via the Greywell Moors Nature Reserve and field paths.

The **Jolly Miller** is a large, mock-Tudor roadside pub at North Warnborough. The menu is extensive and among the fare are baguettes with various fillings, including baked ham, prawns, turkey, various cheeses, paté and hot beef. There is also the classic BLT, or you can opt for a large plate of ham or cheese with salad, home-made coleslaw with crusty bread, vegetarian burger or chilli, whole chicken breast, honey roasted ham with egg and chips, chilli con carne, lasagne, the Jolly Miller breakfast, pizza or jacket potatoes. Real ales include Greene King IPA and Badger Best and Tanglefoot. The Jolly Miller is open all day everyday. Telephone: 01256 702085.

The Walk

With its wide main street lined by handsome 18th century buildings, Odiham is regarded as a jewel among the smaller country towns of southern England. Its focal point is All Saints' church, the largest church in North Hampshire. The impressive pulpit carved with scrolls and vases of flowers is well worth a look, as are the 17th century gallery staircase, 13th century chalk font and 17th century brick tower. Not far from the north side of the churchyard are stocks, together with a whipping post. Inside the churchyard are the graves of several French prisoners from the Napoleonic wars and near the church is a 'Pest House' into which were incarcerated suspected plague sufferers.

① From the centre of **Odiham** follow the **High Street** in an easterly direction. Pass a turning to the **Basingstoke Canal** and turn right just beyond it to join a footpath. Keep ahead, crossing several roads, and make for the outskirts of the town. Pass between wooden panel fencing before reaching a field. Turn left here and skirt the pasture, making for two stiles. Swing to the left of a hedge in front of you and head diagonally across the field to a stile. Turn immediately left, keeping the hedgerow on the left, and head for a footbridge. Maintain the same direction and cross a stile leading out to a road. Turn left and walk along to the A287. (1 mile)

② Cross over to a footpath at **Penarth Stud**, keeping to the left of the buildings. Follow the path ahead over several stiles, then along the edge of a paddock and through the trees to the corner of a large field. Keep close to the left edge until a thatched cottage is reached on the left. Swing left just beyond the cottage and cross a footbridge. Join a drive beyond it and turn right at the T-junction, opposite **Wincombe Cottage**. Follow the lane along to the **Basingstoke Canal**. Cross the waterway at **Broad Oak Bridge**. (1 mile)

Completed in 1794, the Basingstoke Canal is 37 miles long and was originally designed as a major commercial route linking London and Guildford with Southampton. However, the canal's fortunes were never particularly good and eventually the western end was filled in. It was the dawning of the railway era that eventually sounded the death knell. In its heyday the Basingstoke Canal carried vessels loaded with coal, grain, malt, chalk and farm produce. Wayward youths, pickpockets and a variety of other criminals often took a ducking in the canal as punishments for their anti-social behaviour. Restoration work on the canal, involving large numbers of volunteers, began in 1973. Reopened in 1991, much of the waterway is navigable once again.

③ Look for a fork to the left of a bylaws sign and a footpath sign. Keep left here, veering a little to the left when you reach a sign – 'public footpath, no horses'. Continue

KING JOHN'S CASTLE

THE BASINGSTOKE CANAL

through the woodland to a drive and turn left. Pass **Bagwell House** and when you reach the road, turn left to the junction with **London Road**. Turn left to another bylaws sign and then swing right here, passing between trees to reach a stile. Cross a paddock to a double stile and then go slightly left in the next field to another stile. Cross the next field to a double stile in the far boundary, then cross the next one immediately to the right of it. Now begin walking diagonally across a large field, aiming for the arch of a bridge over the **Odiham bypass**. On reaching the field corner, go forward to a stile, then head obliquely up the bank to another stile and turn left to cross the bridge. (2 miles)

④ Turn right to join the **Basingstoke Canal** and walk along to the garden entrance to the **Jolly Miller** at **North Warnborough**. Pass under the road bridge and continue to a swing road bridge by some cottages. Keep ahead on the towpath and before long you reach the entrance to **King John's Castle** on the right. (1 mile)

The castle dates back to 1212 and it was from here that King John set out for Runnymede during the summer of 1215 to sign the Magna

Carta. The following year the stronghold managed to hold out for two weeks against an attack by a French expeditionary force under the Dauphin. King David of Scotland was held captive in the castle for ten years during the 14th century. The sole remaining part of the castle today is its intriguing octagonal-shaped keep – the only one of its kind in the country.

⑤ Resume the walk along the towpath, passing over the **River Whitewater** and beside the remains of a disused lock. Ahead now is the outline of **Greywell Tunnel**, constructed in the 1790s and intended as a short cut to save the canal a circuitous 6-mile cross-country trip. ($\frac{1}{2}$ mile)

The tunnel, which extends for 1,230 yards (getting on for a mile) is the largest known bat roost in Britain, giving it significant ecological importance. Up to 12,500 bats of all native species hibernate here and the tunnel enjoys status as a Site of Special Scientific Interest. The tunnel collapsed on two separate occasions – in 1872 and then again in 1932.

⑥ Follow the path over the tunnel's portal and drop down to the road. Turn right, then left at the junction, and walk through the village of **Greywell**. Continue along the road to the lychgate of **St Mary's church**, pass through a kissing gate and head diagonally over the field. Three-quarters of the way across it, veer right and join a woodland path, crossing the **Whitewater to Greywell Moors Nature Reserve**. Keep ahead through the trees and pass a memorial to the eminent botanist Ted Wallace. Go straight ahead to a stile and then veer obliquely left across a large field to reach the road. (1 mile)

⑦ Turn left for a few paces to a footpath on the right. Follow the path, swinging left after a few paces. Head diagonally across a paddock, cross another stile and maintain the same direction, heading obliquely across the field to the road. Cross it and in the field veer half-right, looking for a stile in the hedgerow, just to the right of three chimneys. Cross over to join a path by a school. Turn right to the road and swing left towards **Odiham**. When the road veers left, go straight ahead into **West Street** and on to the main junction. Cross it and return to the centre of the town. (1 mile)

Date walk completed:

11 JUNE 05

✻ THREE PATHS –
TAKE CENTRE ONE

ITCHEN ABBAS AND MICHELDEVER WOOD

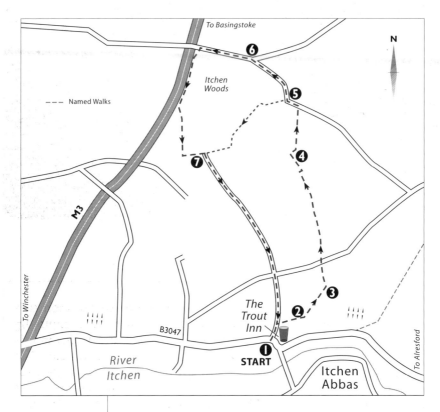

Distance:
6 miles, or 5 miles if you take the short cut south of Itchen Wood

Starting point:
*The Trout Inn at Itchen Abbas.
GR 536328*

Map: OS Landranger 185 or Explorer 132

How to get there: *Itchen Abbas is on the B3047 between Winchester and Alresford. The inn is on the main road.*

THE TROUT AT ITCHEN ABBAS

*F*rom the centre of Itchen Abbas, it is only a matter of moments before you are turning your back on the village and exploring some of Hampshire's loneliest downland country. In the distance is Micheldever Wood – dark and mysterious against the horizon. The noise and speed of the M3 motorway highlights the contrast between the ancient wood and the modern world as you begin the journey back to Itchen Abbas. The return, on a track through farmland and then a quiet lane, gives you splendid views of the Itchen valley.

The **Trout Inn** is situated in the delightful Itchen valley. The rural surroundings have changed little since the summer of 1862 when Charles Kingsley stayed here and wrote part of the children's classic 'The Water Babies'. In those days the inn was known as the Plough. In a letter, Kingsley wrote, 'Oh, the loveliness of this vale and river! It is a happy land round here. I am just starting fishing – day looking perfect: but I don't hope for much, the fish are all feeding at ground ... I have had bad sport enough; so has everyone – but delightful scenery. I am now at the Plough at Itchen.' The river here almost certainly inspired Kingsley to write about the underwater exploits of Tom, the little chimney sweep. The Trout offers a good choice of snacks and main dishes. Real ales include Morland Original and Greene King IPA. The inn keeps traditional hours Monday to Saturday, and is open all day on Sunday. Telephone: 01962 779537.

 The Walk

① From the **Trout** turn right and walk along to the pavement, passing a telephone box. On the right is the village hall. Swing right by some timber and flint cottages and pass **Hazeldene**. On the right is **School Lane**. Pass through railway arches and then turn right by the 30 miles per hour speed limit sign. Walk ahead, keeping to the right of some timber outbuildings, and go up the slope to a stile. Cross the next field by keeping the fence on the right and look for a stile up ahead in the fence. (¹/₂ mile)

② Glance back at this early stage of the walk and you get a good view of the open downland country to the north of **Itchen Abbas**. Large fields and rolling hills make up the scene.

Cross the stile and head diagonally across the field, following the clear path. Make for a stile and gateway and maintain the same direction in the next field. On reaching the field corner, exit to the lane and turn left. (¹/₄ mile)

③ Follow the lane between hedgerows and on reaching a T-junction, with a sign pointing to the right for **East Stratton** and **Northington** and a pair of cottages on the left, go straight on, following the waymarked bridleway. The route here is now a rather rough track with a grassy strip running down the middle. Low-flying helicopters on manoeuvres kept me company on this stretch of the walk. The scenery here also underlines just how remote this corner of Hampshire is. There are few signs of civilisation and, predictably, the surroundings remain much the same, the path maintaining more or less the same direction as it heads for the vast curtain of **Micheldever Wood**, the walk's next objective. (1¹/₄ miles)

④ Eventually the path bends right and then almost immediately left. Continue ahead, with the track now curving to the right by a laurel hedge. After about 70 yards it bends left to a gate. Continue on the straight track down alongside a large field on the left. Make for a gate and keep ahead on a track, cutting between hedges. On reaching a T-junction with another track, turn left and walk down to a right-hand bend. (¹/₂ mile)

⑤ To shorten the walk, keep ahead at this point and rejoin the main walk at point 7 (turning left at the major junction). To complete the main walk swing right at this bend and follow the cycle trail. The track runs up a slope and through trees, a delightful stretch of the walk – particularly in October and November when the autumn colours are glorious. Pass under an overhead bar restricting vehicles and continue between fields and trees. Pheasants may be your only companions; be warned, they can suddenly burst out of the undergrowth and catch you by surprise. (¹/₂ mile)

MICHELDEVER WOOD

A QUIET ROAD ALONG THE ROUTE

The ancient forest here covers about 536 acres of mainly beech woodland with several plantations of mixed oak and conifer. Bluebells thrive in colourful profusion during the spring. Micheldever Wood is acknowledged for several well-preserved archaeological sites, which can be seen from a waymarked heritage trail extending to just over a mile and established by Hampshire County Council and Forest Enterprise. Information boards and explanatory notes help put this peaceful wooded landscape in some kind of historical context and by using your imagination you can picture this area when it was occupied by early settlers.

⑥ Turn left at the road and follow it through woodland. Passing traffic will seem rather intrusive after the peace and tranquillity of the walk's middle stages. The distant hum of traffic on the M3 echoes through the trees as you head west. On the right is a parking and picnic area; if you want to extend the route and follow the waymarked trail, leave the road at this point. To continue the walk, keep ahead, passing a turning on the left for **Itchen Wood**. Just before the M3 bridge turn left to join a tarmac right of way. The odd flash of speeding traffic on the motorway can be glimpsed between the trees, especially in winter. Keep ahead and over to the right you can see a filling station and a motorway café. Continue on the track as far as a waymarked junction and turn left. Follow the cycle way along the edge of dense woodland to a major junction. (1½ miles)

⑦ Turn right, still following the off-road cycle route. Break cover from the trees, follow the track between fields and hedgerows and in the gaps you get wonderful views down into the **Itchen valley**. Keep on the track as it starts to descend and ahead now lie the rambling, timber barns of aptly-named **Lone Farm**. Walk to the right of the outbuildings and join a tarmac lane. Keep to the right of a pair of houses and follow the lane towards **Itchen Abbas**. Pass the regional office of the **Veterinary Laboratories Agency** and walk ahead at the next T-junction, following **Northington Road**. Pass under the railway bridge and return to the **Trout**. (1½ miles)

When you have finished the walk, you might like to explore the Itchen valley further. Numerous footpaths thread their way around the river and out into the open downland of mid-Hampshire. One popular route includes excellent views of Avington Park, a splendid porticoed house built during the 18th century and once the home of John Shelley, brother of the poet. Charles II also stayed here with Nell Gwynn. This is Hampshire river valley scenery at its best.

Date walk completed:

SELBORNE AND FARRINGDON

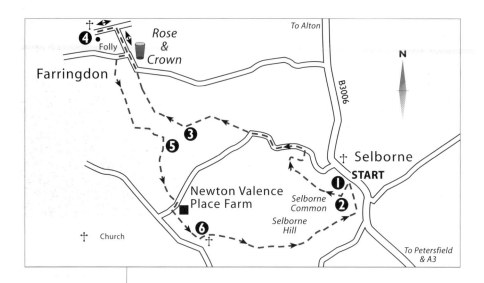

Distance:
7¹/₂ miles

Starting point:
The free public
car park in
Selborne.
GR 743335

Map: OS Landranger 186 or Explorer 133

How to get there: *Make for Alton and then follow the
signs for Selborne, which is situated on the B3006. From
Petersfield follow the A3 north and turn off at the sign for
Selborne. The car park is on the southern edge of the
village.*

EAST HAMPSHIRE FROM THE ZIG ZAG PATH

*E*ast Hampshire, designated an Area of Outstanding Natural Beauty in 1962, covers an area of 148 square miles in a broad swathe from the West Sussex boundary to Winchester. Conservation is the aim here, not recreation, and this walk perfectly illustrates the unique character of this scenic corner of the county. Begin by exploring Selborne's famous chalk hanger, which rises above the village like a slumbering giant. Extensive beech planting took place in the late 18th and early 19th centuries and now trees cover much of the once open chalk downland. From the hanger the walk makes for the village of Farringdon – where you will find Massey's Folly and the delightful Rose and Crown – and then on to Newton Valence before crossing Selborne Common.

Photos of Farringdon and an eye-catching wall map of the world are to be seen inside the attractive, cottagey **Rose and Crown**. There are various daily specials and a snack menu that includes a choice of baguettes with fillings such as Brie and apple, and cheese and chutney. The pleasant enclosed beer garden has wooden tables and chairs, and flowering baskets add a touch of colour to the proceedings during the summer months. Adnams Southwold, Courage, and Greene King IPA are among the real ales on offer. Food is available both lunchtime and in the evening. Telephone: 01420 588231.

 The Walk

Think of Selborne and you immediately think of the 18th century naturalist Gilbert White who lived in the village and was curate here. His father was a barrister and his grandfather vicar of the parish. After school he went up to Oxford and became a Fellow and Dean of Oriel but later returned to his beloved Selborne. White lived at The Wakes, opposite the church, and his old home is now a museum dedicated to the memory of its famous former resident. This glorious corner of Hampshire has long been a favourite haunt of naturalists, many of whom boast a copy of White's classic 'The Natural History of Selborne' among their bookshelves. There are a number of different editions of the book, first published in 1788, and over the years it has been translated into French, Danish, Swedish and Japanese. The original manuscript fetched £100,000 at Christies in 1980. Nothing in this world gave White more pleasure than exploring these secluded paths and woodland glades in search of the local flora and fauna. Jane Austen, who was born 55 years after White in 1775 and lived for a time at nearby Chawton, also knew this area intimately. She may well have followed in White's footsteps, savouring the peace and solitude of this beautiful landscape.

In Selborne's St Mary's church are several reminders of Gilbert White, including a window dedicated to him that depicts St Francis of Assisi feeding the birds. The window has 64 birds in it. The church is about seven centuries old, with a 16th century Flemish triptych over the altar given to St Mary's by White's brother.

① From the car park follow the path signposted '**Selborne Hanger**', pass through a kissing gate at the foot of the hill and begin climbing the **Zig Zag Path**, created by Gilbert White and his brother in 1753 and intended as a short cut to the top of the hill. Before the existence of the path, the climb to the top would have been almost vertical. A seat on the summit allows you to rest and enjoy the spectacular view. With your back to the seat, turn left and go up several steps, veering right in the grassy clearing. ('/4 mile)

② Follow the obvious path through the woods, with the village of **Selborne** and the surrounding downland seen over to the right through a thick curtain of trees. The path gradually descends and when it reaches a junction with a track, turn right. Cut between trees and hedgerows and continue to the road. Turn left and follow the lane as it winds its way through the countryside. At a sharp left bend, go straight on along a bridleway, looking for a gate on the left after about 100 yards. Head diagonally right in the field towards the next pasture, cross a track and follow the path in the same direction towards a solitary tree. Look for a gate in the woodland beyond it and here you should find a bridleway arrow taking you into the trees. (1'/2 miles)

MASSEY'S FOLLY

③ Avoid a footpath on the left and keep ahead on the bridle track as it bends to the right. Further on it narrows to a path cutting between trees and hedgerows. Pass under pylon cables and then take the path on the right for **Farringdon**. Follow it down a gentle slope to a stile, exit to the road and keep left. Turn right by the **Rose and Crown** and follow the lane down to the T-junction. Swing left here and walk along to the church and **Massey's Folly**. (1 $^1/_2$ miles)

It was in 1870 that the Reverend Thomas Hackett Massey, rector of Farringdon church, began work on one of the county's most unusual and eccentric edifices. What Massey built was a red-brick house that was totally at odds with everything else in Upper Farringdon. In other words, it was not in any way conventional or traditional. Over the years some people commented that its highly distinctive Gothic style was inspired by St Pancras station in London. The building boasts 17 bedrooms and it is possible that Massey may have had a theological college in mind when he designed it. Others believed it was intended to be a tearoom for the London-Portsmouth railway.

Massey employed an unknown bricklayer to help him and the two men took 30 years to finish construction work. Massey was prone to irrational outbursts and it was not unknown for him to demolish parts of the building that did not meet with his approval. Over the years, this ornate folly, distinguished by its striking scarlet terracotta panels, has been used as a village school, church hall and general meeting place. Massey died in 1939 and is buried near the porch.

④ Return to the **Rose and Crown**, turn right at the road junction and walk along to a house on the right called **Brownings Orchard**. Turn left here and follow the path as it bends right. Clamber over the stile in the left boundary and cross the field to the next stile. Go half-left in the next field and note the views over to the left – a charming patchwork of fields and hedgerows. Make for a stile at a junction of paths and continue ahead. Pass under pylon cables once again and walk down to a stile. Turn left and follow the field boundary towards woodland. (1 $^1/_2$ miles)

⑤ On reaching a waymark, turn right and follow the track by the pylons. Keep left at the fork and stay on the track all the way to the road. Turn right, then left by an octagonal lodge into parkland. Head up through the park, pass through two wrought iron kissing gates either side of the drive to **Newton Valence Place** and cross a field to pass alongside a holly and laurel hedge.

On reaching a drive, turn left and enter **Newton Valence churchyard**. The 13th century Early English church, which has a magnificent yew tree in the churchyard, was restored in 1871. Gilbert White was curate here for a time. ($1\frac{1}{4}$ miles)

⑥ Keep to the left of the church and leave the churchyard by a grave dating back to the Crimean War. Walk through an avenue of yews and then a copse. Cross a stile and follow the field path towards a curtain of woodland. A hard tennis court edges into view along here. Look for a galvanised gate in the trees, make for a waymark and take the path signposted '**Selborne**'.

Cross **Selborne Common**, where, in the 19th century, cricket was played and cattle once grazed among the trees, and veer right at the waymarked fork. Pass a path on the right and continue. On reaching the corner of the wood, cross a stile and keep ahead round the field edge. Make for a kissing gate in the corner and continue between trees and hedgerows. Ahead is a galvanised gate. Go through it and cross an elongated field to the next gate, then head down the track, passing several cottages. Continue ahead and return to the car park. ($1\frac{1}{2}$ miles)

Date walk completed:

ALRESFORD AND TICHBORNE

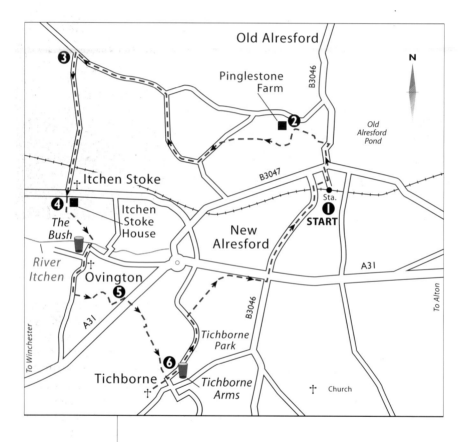

Distance:
9¼ miles

Starting point:
The car park at
Alresford station
(the Watercress
Line). GR 588325

Map: OS Landranger 185 or Explorer 132

How to get there: *Alresford is on the A31, about 7
miles east of Winchester and 14 miles south of Basingstoke.
The walk begins in the fee-paying car park beside the
station at the end of Station Road, off West Street.*

THE BUSH AT OVINGTON

*T*his splendid and very varied route begins in the delightful Georgian town of Alresford, noted for its handsome buildings and enthusiastically supported preserved railway. For those who mourn the passing of steam, the aptly-named 'Watercress Line' offers an opportunity to recapture its magical era on a leisurely journey through picturesque Hampshire countryside. The walk sets out along a stretch of the Wayfarer's Walk and later follows the Itchen Way into Ovington, with its welcoming pub. One of the circuit's lesser-known features is Tichborne, a quiet, secluded village that became the setting for a classic 12th century tale of triumph over adversity.

Hidden away down a quiet lane on the route of the Itchen Way at Ovington stands one of Hampshire's most popular pubs. Looking at its riverside location and charming character bar it's not surprising that the **Bush** draws large numbers of customers. Pews and cosy wintertime fires add to the appeal. Among the fresh, home-cooked dishes, you might find lasagne, beef and ale pie and local trout fillets. There is also an impressive choice of puddings. Real ales include Wadworth 6X, IPA and Farmers Glory and Badger Tanglefoot. The Bush is open every day. Telephone: 01962 732764.

 The Walk

Strictly speaking, there is New Alresford and Old Alresford. Dividing the two is Old Alresford Pond, a reservoir of originally 200 acres built in the 12th century in order to make navigation of the River Itchen possible between Southampton and Bishops Sutton. There are watercress beds here and in the 18th century eels were said to inhabit the watery landscape in great abundance. The name 'New Alresford' suggests the town is modern but in fact there is nothing very new about it. Before the Norman Conquest it was in the possession of the Bishops of Winchester. In the 12th century it was extensively rebuilt by Bishop de Lucy, becoming one of six new towns he planned in Hampshire and Wiltshire.

New Alresford quickly prospered – so much so that it was later considered to be one of the country's most important wool markets, but dark clouds loomed on the horizon. In 1644 the Royalists set the town alight following the Battle of Cheriton nearby. Over 40 years later, in 1689, most of Alresford was burnt to the ground when another fire swept hungrily through it. Because of the fire very few houses seen in the town today were built before that date. However, an impressive feature of New Alresford is the medieval bridge at the bottom of Broad Street.

① From the station car park walk along to **West Street** and turn right, then left into Broad Street. Pass various houses and shops and walk down to a right-hand bend. At this point go straight ahead into **Mill Hill**. Turn left into **Ladywell Lane** and follow the **Wayfarer's Walk**. Pass rows of properties to reach the entrance to **Alre House**. Go straight on along a tarmac path running beside the **River Alre**, a tributary of the **Itchen**. (³/₄ mile)

On the left along here is a peaceful memorial garden dedicated to those who gave their lives in both wars. This secluded plot of land was given to the people of the town by a local resident in 1951. It was rededicated in 2003.

② Pass the ancient 13th century fulling mill, pausing to look at the notice on the wall dated 1253. Don't cross the river here; instead keep to the left bank and turn right on reaching a road. Keep following the **Wayfarer's Walk**, with the river seen on the right through the trees.

Pinglestone Farm is also visible. Pass a kissing gate and continue on the riverside path, crossing the water on several occasions. Pass several houses and some outbuildings and avoid a footpath on the right, running up the hill to the road.

Here and there on this walk, amid the watercress beds, you will see distant figures – workers involved in the process of cultivating and harvesting watercress. This popular, peppery-tasting member of the mustard family is believed to have originated in Ancient Greece. Once known to thrive in

ALRESFORD'S SECLUDED MEMORIAL GARDEN

the open sewers of London, watercress later came to be acknowledged as a rich source of vitamins and minerals.

Follow the well-used path along the field edge to merge with the road and when it bends sharp left, veer right, still following the **Wayfarer's Walk**. Cut between hedges and eventually you reach a junction. Turn left and pass watercress beds on the right. Keep to the left of a remote stone cottage and continue between trees. The scene changes little on this next stretch of the walk and eventually you reach a lane. (2 miles)

③ Turn left here and follow the single-track road between hedgerows. Don't expect it to be busy. I saw little traffic along here last time I did this walk. Cross exposed downland country, with the large, open fields serving as a vivid reminder of modern farming methods in this part of Hampshire. Over to the left in the distance you can just see the buildings of **Alresford**. The lane descends gently to a T-junction at **Itchen Stoke**. On the corner is the very striking **St Mary's church**, designed by the vicar's architect brother in the 1860s and based on the church of Sainte-Chapelle in Paris. (1 mile)

④ Cross over into **Water Lane**, signposted to **Ovington**. Follow the lane down to a footbridge and keep alongside the **River Itchen**, shallow and fast-flowing. **Itchen Stoke House** can be seen over to the left, looking down into the valley. Walk along to a footbridge and cross the river. Make for the road on a bend and on the right here is the **Bush** pub.

To continue the walk, go straight on uphill through **Ovington**, passing **Lane End Cottage** and the church. Note the entrance to **Ovington House** and continue on the road, following it out of the village. Keep alongside a wall enclosing the estate and when you reach the next entrance to **Ovington House**, swing left on the **Itchen Way**. Keep to the left edge of the field and make for a path in the corner, which leads into woodland. (1 1/2 miles)

⑤ Turn left at the road and walk along to the busy A31. Cross over with great care and continue following the **Itchen Way**. Walk ahead in the field, keeping the wood on the right. Make for the field corner and pass through a gap. Swing right into the adjoining pasture, then turn immediately left and skirt the field edge. Head for **Tichborne**, keeping the fence and hedge on the left. When the track becomes enclosed by hedgerows, pass a path on the left which cuts short the walk by taking you directly to the village. The main route continues ahead and just before you reach the road, take a path on the right to Tichborne's 11th century church, **St Andrew's**. Return to the road and turn left. (1½ miles)

The village is well known for the story of the Tichborne Dole. In 1150 Lady Mabella, wife of Sir Roger Tichborne, requested her husband to form a charity to benefit the poor people of the parish. Sir Roger, a man not generally known for his compassion, agreed to provide sick and needy parishoners with a 'dole' of bread annually on 25 March – Lady Day. However, there was one bizarre condition. Sir Roger would only leave to charity the corn in the fields around which his sick and dying wife could crawl in the time it took for a firebrand to burn. Much to his amazement, Lady Mabella rose from her deathbed and crawled around 23 acres of land before the torch's light faded.

To ensure that Sir Roger kept his promise to distribute the bread, Lady Mabella laid a curse on any member of the family who failed to uphold the custom. It would mean that a generation of seven daughters would be born, the family name would disappear and the house would collapse. Not surprisingly, the tradition was maintained but in 1796 a sum of money was substituted for the bread. This turned out to be a wrong move. Part of Tichborne House collapsed and Sir Henry

Tichborne fathered seven daughters.

As a result the original custom of distributing a gallon of flour for adults and half a gallon for children was quickly reintroduced. It has been upheld to this day. Six centuries after the tradition of the dole originated, the Tichborne name was at the centre of a much publicised trial when a man claiming to be Roger Tichborne, the heir to the estate, turned up two years after the real Tichborne had disappeared en route to Australia. The court found the man guilty of fraud and he was sentenced to 14 years in jail.

⑥ Pass the **Tichborne Arms** and a turning to **Tichborne Park** and continue ahead along the road out of the village. Turn right at an intersection and keep on the **Itchen Way**, heading towards **Winchester Lodge**. Pass woodland on the right and follow the obvious path beside farm outbuildings. Cut between fields and eventually the route curves right and runs alongside the A31. Make for the road bridge and turn left towards **Alresford**. Pass the **Cricketers** pub and follow the road to the railway bridge. Walk beneath it and turn right just beyond the Methodist church to join a tarmac path between hedge and fence. Pass beside houses and turn right at the road to reach the car park in front of **Alresford station**. (2¹/₂ miles)

The Mid-Hants Watercress Line is privately run by volunteers. It was officially opened in April 1977, a long awaited but well-deserved reward for its group of enthusiastic supporters. At that time the service terminated at Ropley, 3 miles away, but these days it is 10 miles in length,

extending from Alresford to Alton. The original line, opened in 1865, was 17 miles long and ran between Alton and Winchester. With its gradients, cuttings and embankments, it came to be regarded as an engineering masterpiece. In its day the line provided a vital link for the local watercress industry, supplying much of the rest of the country – hence the name 'Watercress Line'.

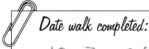
Date walk completed:

10 - 7 - 05

CHERITON AND HINTON AMPNER

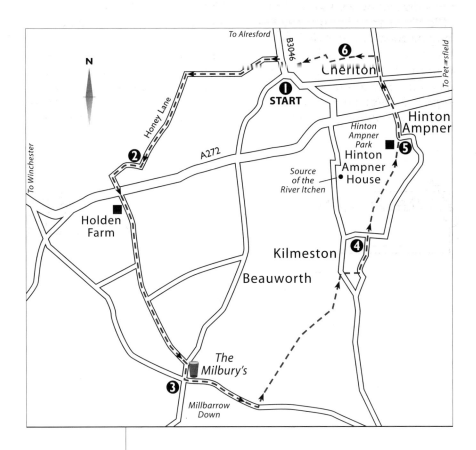

Distance:
9¹/₂ miles

Starting point:
The war memorial
in Cheriton village
centre.
GR 583284

Map: OS Landranger 185 or Explorer 132

How to get there: Cheriton lies to the south of
Alresford, on the B3046, which joins the A272 at New
Cheriton. If you are approaching from Alresford, the war
memorial is on the left, beside the green. There are
parking spaces in the village centre.

REMOTE COUNTRYSIDE IN MID HAMPSHIRE

*L*eaving Cheriton on the delightfully named Honey Lane, this invigorating circuit then follows a section of the South Downs Way to the pub on Millbarrow Down, and returns to the village along the Wayfarer's Walk through Kilmeston. Hard to believe, looking at it today, but a tangled mass of bodies once covered the fields and downland that make up the scene in the closing stages of this wonderfully isolated walk. In the spring of 1644, this was the setting for an important Civil War battle, which is still re-enacted today. Hinton Ampner House amid its peaceful parkland is passed en route to the battlefield.

The 17th century **Milbury's**, which is about a mile south of Beauworth, gets its name from a nearby Bronze Age mill-barrow. The interior of this interesting, characterful pub is dominated by a cosy inglenook fireplace. Heavily wooded walls add to the atmosphere. One of the pub's most famous features is the 250-year-old treadmill originally used to draw water from the 300 ft well in the bar. Food ranges from Ploughman's Platter and sandwiches to roast dishes, baps and baguettes. Cheddar, and Brie and apple, are among the fillings. Real ales include Archers and JCB from Wadworth. The Milbury's is open all day, with food served at lunch-times and in the evenings. Telephone. 01962 771248.

Cheriton is a classic Hampshire village with a pleasant green and a variety of architectural styles. At the heart of the community stands the war memorial; on my travels around Britain, I often stumble upon these sad monuments to a lost generation, still vivid reminders of the sheer waste and futility of war.

① From the war memorial walk along the road through the village, keeping the green on the right. On the left is a house with the letters 'HH' depicted on its front elevation. This was originally an inn, named after the Hampshire Hunt. I recall it still trading in the early 1980s when I passed through **Cheriton** on the newly-opened **Wayfarer's Walk**. Turn left into **Hill Houses Lane** and keep right at the fork by **Colcut Cottage**. Follow the track between trees and hedges, avoid a left

turning and continue on the higher ground. As you approach a large barn, veer left and then head south-west along **Honey Lane**. (1 mile)

② Pass a stile on the left and then swing right just a few paces beyond it. Soon you reach a galvanised gate leading to a field. The path forks beyond the gate and here you keep left, following a section of the **South Downs Way**. On reaching the next **SDW** sign, turn left and follow the track down to the A272. Cross over and go straight ahead to **Holden Farm**. Pass between the buildings, continue ahead at a junction and follow the undulating track to a lane on a bend. Keep ahead, go up the hill and pass **Green Gables** on the right. Turn right at the T-junction, pass alongside the **Milbury's** pub and turn left just beyond it. (3 miles)

③ Follow the road and the parallel path until you reach a sign for the **Wayfarer's Walk** on the left. This represents the start of the return leg of the walk. Cross the stile and go down the field, keeping a fence on your right. Make for a stile and cross into the next field, still following the **Wayfarer's Walk**. Go diagonally across to the corner and then straight ahead in the next field. Head for a stile and follow the enclosed path to a paddock. Cross six stiles to reach the road at **Kilmeston** and take the turning opposite. Take the first footpath on the left, cross more stiles and keep to the right of **St Andrew's church**. (2¹/₂ miles)

④ Turn right at the road, then left at a stile. Follow the path as it runs diagonally across pasture, crossing two more stiles before reaching a gate. Cross the **Itchen Way** at this point and, with the fence on your left, head towards **Hinton Ampner House** nestling peacefully among the trees.

The parkland setting is idyllic and the scene typically English with a village nearby boasting a classically English-sounding name. In fact, the name 'Hinton' comes from the old English word 'heatun' meaning 'village on high ground'. The Ampner in the name is derived from 'almoner', an old word meaning 'giver of alms'. During the Middle Ages the village was one of the Bishop of Winchester's manors and to help provide money for expenses, it was assigned to the office of the almoner of St Swithun's Priory. The present neo-Georgian manor house at Hinton Ampner was expertly rebuilt and restored as recently as 1960, following a fire that almost completely destroyed a fine collection of furniture and

THE MILBURY'S

APPROACHING HINTON AMPNER HOUSE

paintings belonging to the then owner, Ralph Dutton, who became the 8th and last Lord Sherborne. Dutton was returning to Hinton Ampner from a walk when he spotted smoke billowing from the house.

Many different and unusual species of trees were planted around the house and village, including Spanish chestnut, Turkey oak and Norway maple, to provide peaceful walks and pleasing vistas. The 1,640-acre estate of Hinton Ampner is now in the care of the National Trust and the house, together with the grounds, is open to the public during the summer months. Interestingly, the church is located in the grounds of Hinton Ampner House and is of Saxon origin.

Look for a gate in the top corner of the field. During the early months of summer the landscape on this stretch of the walk is plastered with fields of bright yellow oilseed rape. There is often a pungent whiff of it in the air. (1 mile)

⑤ Swing right at the drive and walk down to the A272. Cross over and continue on the track. Go straight on at a crossroads and turn left at the next intersection and barrier, continuing on the clear track. The open farmland and downland here represent the site of a bloody Civil War battle. (1 mile)

With a strong imagination it is possible to picture how this lonely tract of Hampshire countryside might have looked 360 years ago, on 29 March 1644, when it was the scene of an important Civil War battle between the Parliamentarians, led by Sir William Waller, and the Royalist Army, under Sir Ralph Hopton. It became a Parliamentary victory, which halted the Royalist advance towards London. However, the death toll was high, with as many as 2,000 slain. According to popular legend, the blood of the dead and the injured flowed like a river through the surrounding country lanes – a common description applied to many bloody Civil War confrontations. The mounds in this area are reputed to mark the graves of soldiers who took part in the battle.

⑥ At the next junction go straight over to a stile. Take the path round to the right in the field corner and look for a stile on the left. Skirt the field edge and follow the path down into the village of **Cheriton**. Pass the school on the right, veer left at the bridge, then swing left again and return to the war memorial where the walk began. (1 mile)

Date walk completed:

STEEP AND SHOULDER OF MUTTON HILL

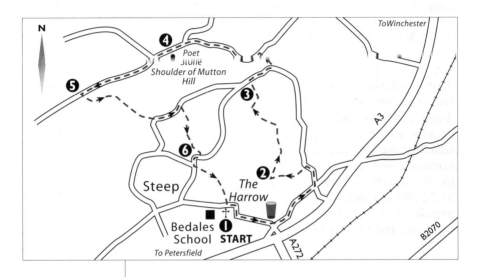

Distance:
6 miles

Starting point:
Steep church.
GR 746253

Map: OS Landranger 197 or Explorer 133

How to get there: *Follow the A272 between Winchester and Petersfield and head north at Stroud for Steep. Go straight over at the crossroads and park by the church.*

THE HARROW - A CLASSIC COUNTRY PUB

*W*ith its spectacular beech hangers and dramatic downland, the countryside of east Hampshire is great for walking. Much of it has thankfully changed little since Edward Thomas, a famous Edwardian poet, strolled here and was moved to write about this glorious landscape in his work. Following in his footsteps, the walk passes the Red House, where he lived for four years, and Berryfield Cottage, his first home in the area. The route also climbs onto Shoulder of Mutton Hill, with its wonderful views, where the sarsen Poet Stone, a memorial to Thomas, is situated.

The **Harrow**, which is just east of Steep and passed early in the walk, is a true gem among country pubs. Run as an inn by the same family since the late 1920s, this 500-year-old building attracts lots of walkers – many of them following the popular Hangers Way. Inside, it is charmingly unspoilt and old fashioned. Character furniture, colourful flower arrangements and various magazines give the impression you might be stepping into someone's living room, tasteful and lived in. Even the outside has a rustic, cottagey feel to it. Food includes the likes of quiche, ploughman's lunch and a variety of sandwiches. Real ales are Ringwood Best, Cheriton Diggers Gold and Pots Ale and Ballards Best. Food is served every day. Telephone: 01730 262685.

The Walk

The partly Norman church of All Saints at Steep includes a Victorian bell turret, a lychgate and a memorial window dedicated to the poet Edward Thomas who features prominently at a later stage of the walk. The window, designed and engraved by Laurence Whistler, was dedicated in 1978, the centenary of Thomas's birth. Whistler was also responsible for the engraved church window at Eastbury in Berkshire, commemorating the life of Helen, Thomas's widow, who spent her final years in the village. Next door to the church is Bedales School, one of Britain's most famous public school institutions. Bedales was founded by John Haden Badley who died aged 102 in 1967. Headmaster Badley was a man of great vision; he was far from conventional. His ideas on education and discipline were quite revolutionary and he was regarded as a controversial figure by his more traditionalist peers. Badley did away with the idea of rigid regimes and traditional doctrine. Instead, he advocated the principle 'spare the rod, spoil the child', believing that children should be given the freedom of thought and expression.

① With the church at **Steep** on your right, walk down the road through the trees and in due course you reach the **Harrow** pub on your left. Walk through the car park, follow the wooded lane at the end and pass a sign 'unsuitable for vehicles'. The sound of traffic on the busy A3 can be heard drifting through the trees. Cross a footbridge over a stream and pass to the left of some pretty timber-framed cottages, avoiding a footpath on the right. Follow the path up the slope and through some trees. The stream can just be seen below, wonderfully secluded and only just visible amid the overhanging boughs of the beech trees. Near here is **Kettlebrook Meadows**, the home of the late Sir Alec Guinness, one of Britain's most versatile film and stage actors. Guinness and his wife moved here in the 1950s, remaining at the house until their deaths in 2000. On reaching a lane at a fork, keep left and follow the narrow lane between trees and hedgerows. Pass a house called **Venables** and some brick and flint buildings on the right. Turn left just a few paces beyond them and follow a track alongside paddocks to a stile. Keep right in the field and make for a second stile in the top boundary. Follow the path as it descends dramatically through the trees and turn immediately right on to a path at the foot of the hill, avoiding the track here. (1 mile)

② Follow the woodland path, cross a stream and make for a cottage in the trees. Cross over the drive and continue on an obvious path. Further on you reach some silos and outbuildings. Look for a fingerpost here. Veer left to a stile and gateway and follow the field perimeter to the corner. Head for a gap in the trees and take the path uphill, along the woodland edge. Go over a stile in the right-hand boundary and cross

SHOULDER OF MUTTON HILL

the field, keeping parallel to power lines. Look for a stile by a metal gate and join a path running up above some woodland. Stay on the enclosed path as far as the lane. (1 mile)

③ Turn right and keep left after about 400 yards, when the lane forks. Turn left after a few more paces to a stile and follow the path between rows of trees, up the tumbling hillside to a stile in the woodland perimeter. Turn left and follow the green lane as it climbs steeply through the trees. Avoid paths on the left and right and eventually you pass a green sign for **Ashford Hangers**, followed in about 200 yards by a barrier. Further on, the walk coincides with a stretch of the 21-mile **Hangers Way**, which runs from Alton to the Queen Elizabeth Country Park, south of Petersfield. (¹/₂ mile)

Climbing to the top of Shoulder of Mutton Hill, it's not hard to see why Edward Thomas loved this area so much. Everything that we appreciate about the English countryside is here and on a fine summer day, with long hours of glorious sunshine and a gentle breeze stirring the trees, there is surely no finer place to be. Although Thomas is regarded as a war poet, essentially his work concentrates on the English landscape. Studying his writing,

you can see how his poetry and prose reflect the unique beauty and magical quality of nature. His passion for the countryside is unmistakable, its changing character and variety of scenery providing a constant source of inspiration.

Thomas's writing also underlines his love of walking, and it wasn't unusual for him to hike up to thirty miles a day, between dawn and dusk. After moving to the village of Steep in 1906, Thomas spent many happy hours roaming this corner of East Hampshire, savouring the glorious beech hangers, the distant downland glimpses and the sheer beauty of the landscape. He knew every inch of this area and one of his favourite haunts was Shoulder of Mutton Hill. From the top the views to the south are magnificent, accurately described by Thomas as 'sixty miles of South Downs at one glance'.

Edward Thomas was born at Lambeth in 1878 and published his first book at the young age of nineteen. In those early years, as well as being a nature writer, he was regarded as something of a literary critic. It wasn't until 1913, with the outbreak of war looming on the horizon, that Thomas began writing poetry. His premature, needless death in the Great War evokes disturbing images of bitter conflict, bloodshed and brutality – the sheer futility of it all. He was killed at the Battle of Arras on the Western Front in the spring of 1917, a man not yet forty years of age, in the prime of life and with everything to live for. Twenty years later, in 1937, the then Poet Laureate Walter de la Mare unveiled a sarsen memorial stone to Edward Thomas on the summit of the hill. De la Mare paid the poet a moving tribute, claiming that 'when he (Thomas) was killed in Flanders, a mirror of England was shattered'.

④ To visit the **Poet Stone**, follow the **Hangers Way** to the left, then straight on when the path veers right after a few paces. Descend steeply to the stone and pause here to savour one of Hampshire's grandest views. Standing on this remote hillside, you can sense the spirit of Edward Thomas and, with a little imagination, picture him exploring this evocative landscape on foot. Return to the main track, turn left and follow the lane. Eventually it runs between houses. Look for the **Red House** and continue down to the road junction. (1¹/₂ miles)

⑤ Turn left here, then immediately left again to follow a sunken bridleway. Descend quite steeply and continue to a fork. Keep right here and rejoin the **Hangers Way**, following it as it crosses a stream and cuts between trees. On reaching the road by a barrier, turn left and pass **Old Ashford Manor**. Walk along to **Berryfield Cottage** on the right, followed by **Ashford Chace**. Continue for about 60 yards and turn right at another sign for the **Hangers Way**. Follow the track and as it bends right by a private sign, veer left to follow a woodland path. After the path bends right and left, turn right and go down some steps to a waterfall. (1¹/₂ miles)

⑥ At the road beyond it, keep right and walk along to a right-hand turning. Veer left here, passing through a kissing gate. Turn right and skirt the field to reach a plank bridge and stile in the corner. Cross it into woodland and follow the path to a small playing field. Head across the grass and emerge at the road opposite **Steep church**, where the walk began. (¹/₂ mile)

Date walk completed:

BISHOP'S WALTHAM AND THE PILGRIMS' TRAIL

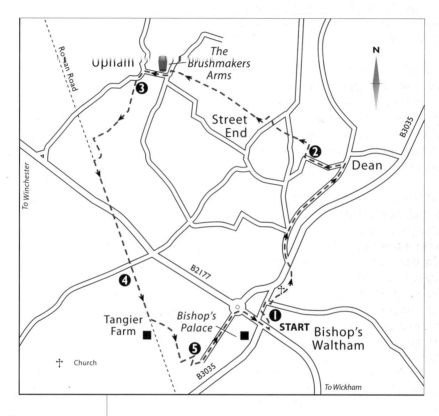

Distance:
9 miles

Starting point:
The car park at the junction of Bank Street and Brook Street in Bishop's Waltham.
GR 554176

Map: OS Landranger 185 or OS Explorer 119

How to get there: Bishop's Waltham is on the B2177 between Wickham and Winchester.

THE BRUSHMAKERS ARMS

*A*ncient palace ruins and a cross-Channel pilgrimage route, forgotten for 400 years, help to illustrate Hampshire's fascinating and colourful history on this walk around the old town of Bishop's Waltham. According to the *Dictionary of British Place Names*, the name of the town means 'bishop's homestead in a forest'.

The **Brushmakers Arms** at Upham dates back about 400 years and was probably built as a private house. To those who are visiting for the first time, the most striking aspect of this very popular country pub is its rather unusual name. This is where, 200 years ago, brushmakers used to meet while plying their wares in the area. Inside, you'll find an L-shaped bar, a low ceiling and various other interesting character features. The menu is very extensive, with a good range of snacks, including sandwiches, basket meals and jacket potatoes. More substantial fare ranges from battered cod to steak. On Sunday the menu is restricted to a traditional roast. There are no permanent real ales but Ringwood Best is one of the regular favourites. Telephone: 01489 860231.

The Walk

Thankfully, the centre of Bishop's Waltham has retained much of its charm and character over the years. Many of its streets are lined with quaint Georgian houses. The town is still remembered for having the only privately owned bank in Britain, before it was sold to Barclays in the early 1950s. The Bishop's Waltham and Hampshire Bank was founded in 1809 and was later known as Gunner's Bank.

Bishop's Waltham is also famous for its ruined palace, built as a medieval retreat by the powerful Bishop Henry de Blois around 1135 and now in the care of English Heritage. William of Wykeham died here in 1404. The ruined state of the palace is in sharp contrast to the parish church of St Peter, which has been extensively restored over the centuries. Its most eye-catching feature is the early 17th century tower, which is large and squat with Tudor-style windows. Rising above it is the staircase turret.

① From the car park, cross over into **Bank Street** and then turn left into **St Peter's Street**. Cross the churchyard to the road and veer left. Head for the B3035 and take the turning almost opposite (signposted **Alresford** and **Cheriton**). Keep right at the next junction for **Dean** and follow **Dean Lane**. Take the first left turning on reaching **Dean** and walk along to a sharp left-hand bend. (2¹/₂ miles)

② Turn right here and walk along to a stile and footpath on the left. Skirt the field, keeping the fence on the left, and look for a stile in the top boundary. Cross the road to a stile and aim half-right in the field, passing under power lines. Head for two stiles with a field between and cross the road to **Street End Farm**. Pass the farm outbuildings and stay on the grassy track as it bends left and then right. Eventually you reach the field corner. Cross a stile and descend steeply to the next one. Follow the track and keep to the right of the farm. Swing left at the road, then right at the fork by a pond (signposted '**Winchester**'). Pass the turning to the **Brushmakers Arms** on the right and walk along to the **Upham** village sign. Head through the village and swing left into **Oak Close**. (2 miles)

The history of the Bishop's Palace is varied and interesting. 250 years after the death of William of Wykeham, at the height of the Civil War, it was captured by Parliament with the then bishop holed up inside with 200 Royalist soldiers. But he was lucky, managing to flee unharmed in a dung cart. Cromwell's men subsequently attacked the palace, leaving it in the ruinous state you see today. Having acquired it in 904 AD, the Bishops of Winchester finally vacated Bishop's Waltham in the 1860s.

THE RUINS OF THE BISHOP'S PALACE (WINCHESTER CITY COUNCIL)

③ When the road curves right by some houses, continue straight ahead along a path. Cross two stiles and follow a track running south-west across fields. Keep going until you come to a galvanised gate on the left. Follow the **Pilgrims' Trail** waymarks, cutting between woodland on the left and a plantation on the right. Swing right at the end of the wood and cross the field to a stile. Turn left and make for the stile in the field corner. Follow the route of a Roman road out across the field, making for a stile in the distant boundary. Cross the lane and go straight ahead to the B2177. Make for a gap in the hedge opposite and continue on the walk, following the path through trees to reach a kissing gate. Skirt the next field by keeping to the right boundary, head for the next gate and just beyond it you reach a lane. Turn left and make for the next junction. (2 miles)

The Pilgrims' Trail, linking the shrine of St Swithun in Winchester Cathedral with the Mont St Michel monastery in Normandy, was officially opened to commemorate the new millennium, the occasion marked by a group of fourteen pilgrims making the 155-mile cross-Channel journey to honour the Archangel St Michael. The pilgrimage route was once used by Miquelots – pilgrims who revered the Archangel. The pilgrims on the inaugural walk crossed the Channel between Portsmouth and Cherbourg, arriving at Mont St Michel at the end of September 1999. They carried with them 'passports' that were stamped at cathedrals and holy sites along the way. The original route was abandoned after the Reformation but the new trail has been cleared and signposted for today's pilgrims.

④ Cross over to a stile to the right of a drive, then go diagonally across the field. Pass into the next field through the wide gap and make for the next stile. Walk to the right of a nursery and cross two stiles. Continue ahead for about 100 yards, in line with pylons, and swing right to a footbridge. Turn left and head for **Tangier Farm**. Cross a stile to a track, turn left for several paces and then right at a stile and gate. Walk ahead across the fields until you reach a footbridge on the right. Turn left at this point to two stiles. (1 1/2 miles)

⑤ Go diagonally right in the field and join a track. Keep right and go up to a junction. Turn sharp left, pass a bungalow and when the track curves right, go straight ahead through a kissing gate. Follow the disused railway to the main road and turn right. Pass a petrol station to reach the **Bishop's Palace**. Follow the road to the next roundabout, swing left into the **High Street**, then left again into **Cross Street**. Go right at the junction with **Brook Street** and return to the car park. (1 mile)

Date walk completed:

19 JUNE 05

MEONSTOKE, DROXFORD AND THE WAYFARER'S WALK

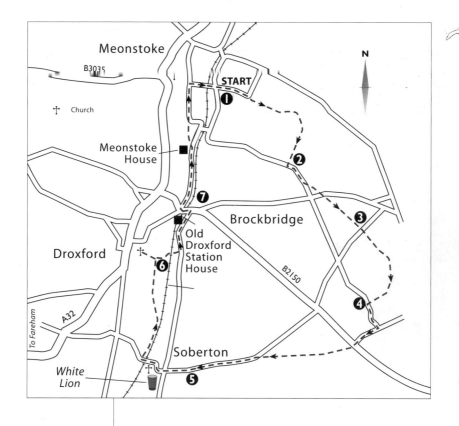

Distance:
8¹/₄ miles

Starting point:
Meonstoke village hall car park. GR 617202

Map: OS Landranger 185 or OS Explorer 119

How to get there: *Meonstoke is on the A32 between Alton and Fareham. Turn off the main road at the Bucks Head pub and follow the sign for Meon Hall and Pound Lane.*

THE VILLAGE OF MEONSTOKE

*A*t the heart of this walk lies some of Hampshire's most glorious countryside – a rich mix of open downland and picturesque river valley. Three-quarters of the way round, following the route of the 70-mile Wayfarer's Walk, we reach the village of Droxford. It was here that Izaak Walton fished in the River Meon, reflecting that the valley 'exceeds all England for swift, shallow, clear, pleasant brooks and store of trout'. His daughter married the local vicar. Near this spot, a new trail follows the trackbed of the disused 22½-mile Meon Valley Railway. This ran from Fareham to Alton and was in service between 1903 and 1955. If you prefer, as an alternative to the Wayfarer's Walk, you could join the Meon Valley Trail at Soberton and rejoin the main route at Brockbridge just north of Old Droxford Station House.

The **White Lion** at Soberton is a fascinating old pub, with plenty of charm and character. The building dates back to the 17th century, when it was a private house. Built-in wooden wall seats, beams and old-fashioned décor add to the appeal of the place. The White Lion is open all day, with food served throughout opening hours, and there is also an à la carte restaurant on Tuesday to Saturday. In the bar you'll find an extensive menu, featuring the likes of baguettes, crêpes, home-cooked pies, soup, bangers and mash and even water buffalo cheeseburger. Real ales include Morland Old Speckled Hen, Bass, Wadworth 6X and White Lion Bitter. Telephone: 01489 877346.

The Walk

① On leaving the car park, turn right and follow the lane. When you reach a sharp left bend, veer off to the right for a few yards towards a private drive sign. Branch left at this point and cut between the trees. Further on you begin a moderate climb between trees and fields before dropping down between hedges to the road. (1¼ miles)

② Turn left, pass a transmitter on the right, and turn left just beyond it at a gateway. Head obliquely right in the pasture, making for a line of trees. Negotiate two stiles either side of a minor road and cross a large field to a barn. Keep to the left of it, cutting along the field edge to reach the road. (1 mile)

③ Cross over to a white gate. Follow the drive ahead and shortly you take a parallel path on the right. Look out for several paddocks and a cedar tree along here. Pass through a gate and follow a wide grassy path heading in a south-easterly direction. The path becomes a track further on, skirting woodland. When you arrive at a fork, with a gate seen on the right, keep right and follow the path between trees. Turn right when you reach the next track and follow the waymarked permitted route. Turn left at the next junction and walk down the track in the direction of farm buildings. Turn left on reaching them and cut through the wood. On reaching a path crossing the track, swing right to the road. (1 mile)

④ Turn left, then right at the T-junction to follow a minor road passing houses and woodland. Cross the B2150 to a stile and join a waymarked path skirting the wood. Beyond the trees, head out across the pasture to two stiles, then go diagonally across the next field to a ladder stile giving access to the road.

Turn left here, pass the **Soberton** village sign and turn right at a track, avoiding a galvanised gate and stile on the extreme right. (2 miles)

⑤ Take the track to **Soberton** and turn right at the road. Pass the **White Lion**, then swing immediately left into the churchyard. On leaving it turn left at the gate and follow the path along to the road. Turn left and follow the lane downhill to the route of the **Wayfarer's Walk**. Turn right and follow the trail through the picturesque valley, crossing three stiles to reach a footbridge. (1 mile)

⑥ Turn left here to visit **Droxford**. To continue the walk, turn right and go up the field slope to a kissing gate. Avoid the path on the left and head straight on to the next gate, veering left to a galvanised gate and wooden gate. Follow the track over the disused **Meon Valley Railway** to the road and turn left, passing a house on the left which used to be Droxford station.

The clues are all here – the name is Old Droxford Station House and the canopy above the station platform is just visible, attached to the back of the property. In case

DOWNLAND ABOVE THE MEON VALLEY

you miss this, read the plaque attached to the post box at the entrance to the house, proclaiming that 'in a special train at this station, the Rt Hon Sir Winston Churchill MP, then Prime Minister of the United Kingdom, spent some days making crucial decisions with his staff prior to the invasion of Europe on D-Day June 6, 1944'.

⑦ At the T-junction beyond the station building, turn left and avoid a turning to **Meonstoke**. Look for a drive on the right and follow it to **Brockbridge Cottage**. Aim for a waymark and fingerpost at the end of the garden and join a woodland path, following it to a drive. Keep ahead to the road and make for the entrance to **Meonstoke House**. Take the path on the left just beyond it and cut between fences. Pass alongside a school, join the road on a bend, and continue ahead through **Meonstoke**. When the road bends left, veer right at the sign for **Meon Hall** and **Pound Lane**. Follow the road to the right and return to the village car park. (2 miles)

Date walk completed:

ON JUNE 05

HAMBLEDON AND THE CRADLE OF CRICKET

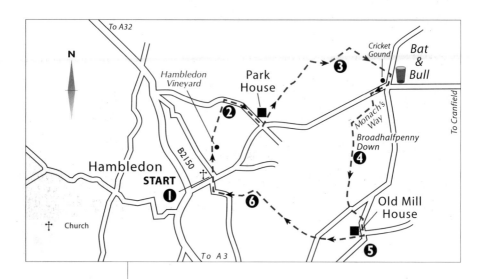

Distance:
8 miles

Starting point:
Hambledon village
centre.
GR 646151

Map: OS Landranger 185 and 196 and Explorer 119

How to get there: *Hambledon lies to the north of Portsmouth, on the B2150 road between the A3 and the A32. There is room to park in the village centre.*

* AT BOUNDARY BE CAREFUL THERE ARE 2
POSSIBLE ROUTES ABOUT 150 YDS APART TAKE
FURTHEST.

** PAST SCOTLANDS COTTAGE TRACK LEADS TO STILE
BUT IS AT END OF TRACK AND TO ONE SIDE AND
IS COVERED IN VEGETATION.

⊗ BIT CONFUSING (GOT LOST HERE) SHOULD
GO INTO FIELD OPPOSITE, NOT UPHILL.

PICTURESQUE HAMBLEDON

*A*ccording to Arthur Mee's book on Hampshire, 'Hambledon has a warm place in the heart of every Englishman'. Mee is referring to the village's status as the home of the game of games – cricket. Later, we'll be visiting the Bat and Ball and Broadhalfpenny Down, which played a crucial role in the early history of this quintessentially English sport.

The **Bat and Ball**, on the Clanfield road about 2 miles east of Hambledon, dates back to about 1730 when it was also used as a cricket pavilion and clubhouse. The landlord at that time was Richard Nyren who was considered to be the best all round cricketer of his day and whose life was dedicated to the game. Sandwiches, jacket potatoes, bangers and mash and liver and bacon feature on the menu, as do rib-eye steak, various fish dishes and traditional Sunday roast. Food is served every day and there is a popular beer garden. Real ales include George Gale HSB, GB and Butser. Telephone: 02392 632692.

The Bishop of Winchester granted Hambledon a weekly market in the 13th century and looking at it today, a sprawling commuter village of Georgian and timber-framed houses sitting snugly in a shallow Hampshire valley beneath rolling hills, beechwoods and chalk downland, it is hard to imagine it was once a prosperous, fast-growing town. James I granted the Bishop of Winchester the right to hold fairs here early in the 17th century, and the toll paid to the lord of the manor for setting up the booths was a broad halfpenny. The church, enlarged several times, was restored in the 19th century. It is often described as a textbook example of how an English parish church has been extended and altered between Saxon and medieval times. There is evidence of Saxon work in the walls of the nave. In his 'Rural Rides', William Cobbett describes Hambledon church as being pretty nearly as large as that at Farnham in Surrey.

Hambledon has an interesting connection with two monarchs. Charles II fled here as a fugitive after the Battle of Worcester. He slipped unseen into the village on 13th October 1651 and stayed the night at a cottage on the road to Denmead, escaping to Sussex the next day and then travelling on to France. There was a reward of £1,000 for his capture. The second king to visit Hambledon was George VI who came to the village in May 1944 to inspect the troops prior to the invasion of Normandy the following month. The parade took place in Chestnut Meadow, opposite the cottage where the fugitive king had spent the night nearly 300 years earlier.

① From the centre of **Hambledon**, take the turning opposite the grocery, walk towards the church and follow the road to the right in

THE CRICKET MEMORIAL WHICH FACES THE BAT AND BALL PUB

front of the entrance to the churchyard. Bend left along the lane and then take a path on the right immediately before the village school. Pass alongside the schoolyard, then swing left at the corner. Keep the school on your left and head diagonally right, following the path across a field to a hedge to the left of a grove of trees. Keep the hedge on the right and descend the slope to reach the road. (1 mile)

Over to the right lies Hambledon Vineyard. With soil not dissimilar to the Champagne region of France, Hambledon used to be one of the largest vineyards in the country with its vines yielding 8,000 to 10,000 bottles of white wine a year. The vineyard, which comprised five acres on Windmill Down, was established in the early 1950s by Major General Sir Guy Salisbury-Jones, a distinguished soldier who fought in the First World War and who later became Marshal of the Diplomatic Corps. It was suggested to him one day that the sunny south-facing slopes adjoining his Hambledon home would be put to very good use as a vineyard. After a visit to Burgundy to seek the advice of experts in the field, Sir Guy returned home having acquired 4,000 vines during his trip. He soon turned the idea into reality.

② Turn right, pass a turning for **Chidden**, make for the T-junction and go left towards **East Meon** and **Clanfield**. Pass **Park House** and then veer left at the footpath sign and the **Wayfarer's Walk** waymark. Look for a gate and follow the track ahead, passing alongside a brick and flint wall on the right. Skirt the field and cut through a wood. Almost at the far end, where there are fields ahead, look for a waymark and veer left to join a path. Stay on the **Wayfarer's Walk**, emerge from the woodland and head diagonally right across the field. Don't pass through the boundary on the far side; instead, turn right and walk along the perimeter of the field to a waymark and a gap in the trees. Follow the path through the wood to the next field, swing right and make for the road. (2 miles)

③ On reaching it, cross over into the field opposite and continue ahead to a stile. Turn right and cross three stiles to the road. At this point turn right and walk along to the **Bat and Ball** pub, pausing here for a well-earned rest!

Opposite the Bat and Ball is the famous cricket memorial, marking the site of the ground of the Hambledon Cricket Club circa 1750–1787. Originally the game was played with two forked sticks as stumps. A third stump was eventually introduced and the width of the bat came to be recognised as 4¼ inches. The club

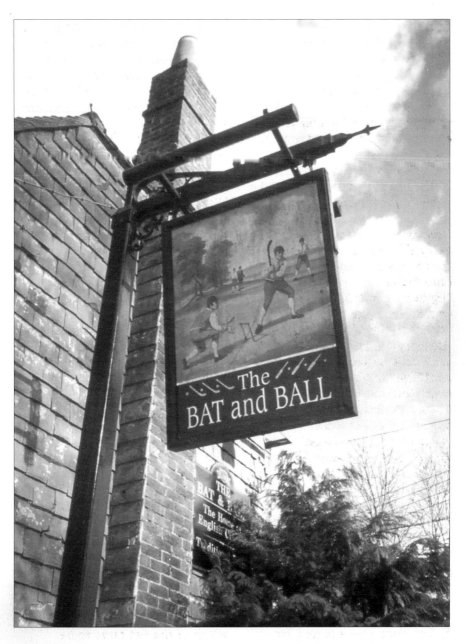

THE BAT AND BALL PUB SIGN

was responsible for laying down the rules of the game as we know it today and this is where it changed from being a village pastime to a national institution. By the end of the 1780s Hambledon was considered too remote a setting for its headquarters and so cricket moved to a more central location in the heart of London. The more famous Marylebone Cricket Club attracted many of the best players of the day and, in no small measure, helped to raise the profile of the game.

On leaving the pub, turn left to the junction, then swing right towards **Fareham**. Walk along to a stile on the left, opposite a junction, cross it and climb the slope, keeping to the right-hand path. Cross the stile at the top, turn right and follow the track across **Broadhalfpenny Down** towards **Scotland Cottage**. This blustery high ground conveys something of the contrast between Hampshire's remote countryside and its varied coastline. Glimpsed here and there are the island city of **Portsmouth**, **Langstone Harbour** and the grey ribbon of the **Solent** merging with the horizon. (1³/₄ miles)

④ Veer left immediately beyond **Scotland Cottage** and join a path leading to a track. Make for a stile and head down the field. Pass into the adjoining field and, after a few paces, cross another stile which leads to a track. Cross over it and follow the path ahead up the slope over three stiles and then up a short flight of steps to the road. Turn right and pass **Harrowgate House**. Follow the lane along to **Old Mill House** and cross a stile beyond it. (1 mile)

⑤ Take the path, cross three stiles and descend the slope to a meeting of paths and tracks. Walk ahead up the field slope to a track, cross it and keep the hedge on your right. Descend into a hidden fold, rise to the far side and then head for the trees ahead. Pick your way between them and continue ahead in the next field. In wet conditions, keep to its left-hand edge. Cross a track and then make for the next stile ahead. (1¹/₂ miles)

⑥ Turn left and pass the buildings of a stud farm to reach a stile. Cross it, then, on reaching a drive, turn left away from the farm. Veer right after a few paces to join a path. Follow the **Wayfarer's Walk** and the **Monarch's Way** to reach a fork by the drive to **Rose Cottage**. Take the left turning and descend the hill into **Hambledon**. Soon the village edges into view. Follow the road back to the start of the walk. (³/₄ mile)

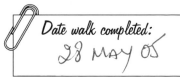

Date walk completed:
28 MAY 05

SOUTHWICK AND PORTSDOWN HILL

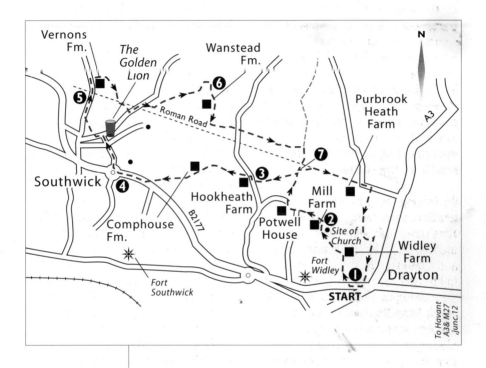

Distance:
10 miles

Starting point:
The car park on Portsdown Hill. GR 664064

Map: OS Landranger 196 or OS Explorer 119

How to get there: *From the M27 at junction 12, head north on the A3. Take the second turning for the B2177 (Portsdown Hill) and follow it towards Southwick. Approaching from the north, take the first turning for the B2177 off the A3. Pass the George pub and the car park is along on the left.*

THE HISTORIC GOLDEN LION AT SOUTHWICK

A spectacular and very varied walk, starting with magnificent views across Portsmouth, Britain's only island city. Very quickly you head north, away from the coast, and the sharp contrast between Portsmouth's urban wasteland and the peace and quiet of the countryside is immediately apparent. During the mid 19th century this area was on alert when there was a real fear of invasion from the French who might have invaded this country further east in Sussex and then made an assault on Portsmouth from the north. Parts of this walk give an insight into the kind of landscape and terrain the enemy would have encountered. At Southwick you can visit, by appointment (telephone: 02392 284235), the famous map room which played such a vital role in D-Day and the final outcome of the Second World War.

In the days leading up to D-Day the saloon bar of the **Golden Lion** at Southwick – a classic character pub – was used as an unofficial officers' mess. Field Marshal Montgomery drank grapefruit juice while General Dwight D. Eisenhower consumed half pints of bitter. The beer he drank here was brewed in the brewhouse at the rear of the inn. Today's menu is no doubt a little more extensive than it was in those far-off, dark days. Typical examples include bangers and mash, ham, egg and chips, steak and kidney pudding, battered cod and a range of sandwiches and jacket potatoes. Real ales include those locally produced from the Oakleaf Brewery, plus various guest beers. Telephone: 02392 379134.

Because of its vulnerability to attack, Portsmouth has been fortified throughout history to such an extent that no other port can claim to be as well protected against invasion. A prime example of the city's fortification is Portsdown Hill, with its six polygonal forts strategically sited at intervals of between 1 and 1½ miles. It was a royal commission in 1860 that recommended this area should be better defended against attack. The Cabinet was split over the idea, and Gladstone, Chancellor of the Exchequer at the time, threatened to resign. Lord Palmerston, however, the then Prime Minister, was convinced the defence work should go ahead and a decision was made to proceed. The low position of the forts and the way they easily blended into the contours of Portsdown Hill meant that from the north they were hardly visible at all. This was an intentional ploy to deceive the enemy, should the French come ashore in Sussex and attempt to attack from the rear. About 7 miles long, stretching from Bedhampton to Fareham, the hill was also a vital link in communication, enabling signals to be transmitted between Whitehall and Portsmouth.

① Make for the eastern end of the car park and cross the B2177 to a concrete track. Follow it down towards **Widley Farm** and turn left immediately before a bungalow. Take the track to a stile by two gates and head diagonally across the field towards **Mill Farm**. Turn right at the stile and walk along the lane to reach the site of the parish church of **St Mary Magdalen**. (1 mile)

② Follow the lane until it bends left. Turn left here over a stile, crossing

NEAR SOUTHWICK